# The Stress Gremlins©

## Developing Strategies for Stress

## By

## Ann McCracken

Published 2005 by abramis

www.abramis.co.uk

ISBN 1-84549-020-7

Printed and bound in the United Kingdom

Typeset in Palatino 12/26

abramis is an imprint of arima publishing

arima publishing
ASK House, Northgate Avenue
Bury St Edmunds, Suffolk IP32 6BB
t: (+44) 01284 700321

www.arimapublishing.com

## Acknowledgements

*One of the Chapters is headed 'No person is an Island' and I have had many wonderful people who have supported me in the writing of this book - my colleagues and friends at stressmanagers.co.uk, Sally Carpenter, Jonathan Pearce and Mandy Perry have all given me encouragement when I really needed it. Andrew Hutley, my friend and husband has been the wind beneath my wings.*

*Some of the assessments have been adapted from the Spectra Peak Performance Programme with kind permission of Denise Williams of The Business International Partnership, Cambridge.*

*The gremlin concept has been brought to life by Clive Francis of the Cartoon Cupboard for which grateful thanks are expressed.*

# Introduction

The potential for stress is universal. Whether you believe in it or not, your body will be affected by too much or too little emotional pressure, the natural internal balances will be undermined and if you ignore the early signs, physical or psychological illness will result. This stunning statement has repercussions in organisations, families, education, health and social services.

People fascinate me. I can remember many years ago sitting looking down a microscope whilst doing my research for my post graduate degree in Immunology and observing some very attractive bacteria which I had just stained and thinking "you are very nice, but I prefer people".

It has taken me many years to fulfil that emerging passion. After training as a stress management practitioner, I began working with people who were showing indications of stress. I learned how individual and diverse, human reactions to excessive pressure can be. This is one of the reasons why it has been difficult to define stress in the last few years. Another reason is that many of the indications of a 'stressed' individual do not conform to a standard pattern of known illness. This is because the whole body is affected by excessive pressure and aches and pains are often combined with skin disorders, anxiety and headaches. The collection of disparate symptoms were often described as 'a virus' in the past and are now often attributed to the generic term, stress.

A person in such a condition does not feel good. Their ability to cope is drastically reduced, their resilience is depleted and their self-esteem begins to plummet. Both mind and body are affected. Some are able to identify the causes and change their response to them or reduce them completely. This allows the individual to recover and nourish themselves – in both body and mind. Many people are unable or unwilling to recognise the cause(s) of their stressed state and soldier on. Eventually this will result in a recognised illness, which is sadly a side effect of stress.

This book is the result of my experiences working with thousands of clients and sharing their successes as they climbed the ladder back to well being. All the strategies and tips have been trialed with clients as well as student practitioners whose feedback was extremely helpful. The strategies are many and varied, just like the people they are designed to support.

The early chapters introduce the concepts, causes and outcomes of stress as well as a fun model to explain the insidious development of chronic stress. The main part of the book explores how individuals vary immensely in their emotions, reactions to these emotions and ability to appreciate how these affect their body and mind. There are many case studies from all walks of life to help the reader to identify with other peoples' experiences and to learn about their outcomes. The final part of the book encourages readers to assess all their risk of stress and to take control by minimising their key stress factors.

In my practice I encourage my clients to take a wide view of their life and take into account all the factors affecting them. This is what I have shared with the readers in this book. By giving each factor a weighting, clients can then integrate all their life factors and make inspired choices of how the balance needs to be changed or not.

# Ann McCracken

# Chapter 1

# The concept of stress

- why stress now?

- is stress real or imagined?

- body reactions

- the attitude to stress

- stress warnings

- stressed or busy?

- gremlins

- causes of stress

- the importance of awareness

=============================

"I'm not going to be able to make the Neighbourhood Watch meeting tonight," James said to Debbie during a hurried mobile phone conversation. "Well, after the burglary, you are the one they want to talk to" she said. "I'm just too busy here at work and I must get this report off by e mail tonight...sorry........."

Debbie went to the meeting and it brought back some of the horror of last week when they had returned home after a rare evening out with friends, to find the back door open and their TV, DVD, computers and jewellery gone. Her neighbours wanted to know if the police had got any further with the case but as far as she knew, no one had been arrested and nothing had been recovered. She had such a sense of violation, knowing that someone had been rooting around their house and personal things. She had been offered a chat with someone from Victim Support but felt she had enough to do right now. The insurance claim was turning out to be difficult, as she could find no receipts for the jewellery. At least she could show them the credit card statements for most of the other things.

=============================

So what does 'stress' mean to you?

You can probably see some of the pressures on James and Debbie in the above scenario and may relate to James's demanding work life or Debbie's sensitivity.

Is stress different at work from how you experience it at home? What are you describing when you use the word stress?

Stress is used in many contexts and means different things to different people. The search for a definition has revealed a huge variety of descriptions. For example:

As defined in the Oxford English Dictionary stress is:
*"mental, emotional or physical strain or tension"*

As defined by an engineer, stress is:
*a force producing a change of shape or volume.*

The Health and Safety Executive (HSE) define stress as:
*the adverse reaction people have to excessive pressures or other types of demand placed on them"*

These definitions all suggest that stress is the result of some type of pressure.

Human stress has come to be associated with pressure created by changes in culture, demands, expectations, environment and relationships. We all react to obvious as well as subtle pressures with some type of emotional response. It could be annoyance, delight, apprehension, fear or some other response. This creates a biochemical reaction in the body which will continue to build up if the pressure is constant or increased. The result is an imbalanced system and the outcome is minor or eventual serious illness.

This means that :

**'stressed' is not a good place to be.**

# Why stress now?

Stress is the result of a build up of too many or too few demands on a person. The development of DNA profiling, means that most people know that we are all slightly different due to genetic variation but we are also deeply affected by our life experiences. These variations mean that some people can handle more pressure and change than others.

In the last 50 years, global changes and life expectations have affected us all by increasing pressure and demands.

## Pace of Life

Recognise that life pressures today are very different to those 30 years ago

Sometimes I feel that the earth is spinning faster than ever before! There always seems so much to do and so little time to do it. My grandfather and my parents both had such a different life – it was slower, insular, cleaner, shorter, organic and, for the first time in our society, damaged by a war with global overtones. After the Second World War the speed of life seemed to gradually change and city life became more frantic. This is now spreading to the urban areas and one has to go to the extremely depopulated areas to find tranquillity. It is interesting to note that such tranquillity can be just as challenging for some as fast city life is for others.

## Education

Not just in Britain, but in most countries of the world, education has been made available to everyone. The general level of knowledge has been extended throughout society. Education is no longer gender biased and women have taken a greater part in the workforce at all levels. This has created another pressure within the home as both partners, who are also often parents, are working and children are cared for in nurseries and after school groups There are greater expectations on young people to gain educational qualifications and greater expectations of the education system itself. Young people are now very aware of the pressures from parents, teachers and their own expectations.

## Class

Before the Second World War there was a very clear class structure in Britain. There were limited opportunities to move from working to middle or upper class and this has changed greatly. Entrepreneurs have led the way, money and titles are no longer synonymous and education has opened doors and minds.

## Social

Standards of living and personal expectations have been raised in a consumer-led society. Housing is changing and the advent of washing machines, dishwashers, vacuums, fridges and freezers have revolutionised household activities and released women into the workplace. In many homes, chores are shared and some choose to outsource many domestic chores. This can have a beneficial effect of reducing some pressure.

## Work

The greatest change in the workplace is the lack of job security. Although the 19th & 20th Century saw much unemployment in traditional industries, the increase in clerical and technical posts brought long term job security and 'a job for life' was not unusual. There was limited movement of employees and most employees worked within a short distance of their home. In the last 50 years there has been a greater increase in workforce mobility. Mergers and takeovers have increased often resulting in short term contracts. Greatly increased responsibilities have also been noted with one person now being responsible for two or more jobs. Relocation has forced people to move far away from family support. Commuting locally, nationally and internationally has increased. Public services have been privatised creating very different cultures within them. Even the 'safe' jobs like teaching and civil service are witnessing redundancy and short term contracts. It is fair to say that some people find these changes releasing and motivating, allowing variation and independency. There has been an increase in self employment which has its own unique pleasures and pressures.

Many people tell us they feel insecure on short term contracts because they are committed to fixed term mortgages. Some have chosen redundancy or just left employment after disillusionment or 'burn out' to set up as sole traders or small businesses, often changing career path. This is the route followed by myself and my colleagues after retraining as stress management practitioners.

## Technology

> Understand change
> and make it work
> for you

This is the area where the speed of change has been phenomenal. The introduction of the computer chip into every area of life has revolutionised the workplace, hospitals, schools, entertainment and homes. In the early stages it brought pressure to learn new skills and now pressure comes from the change in speed that technology has created as well as when it fails to work. Office rage has been described in national papers when employees and home users react to technology failure.

In a society, the results of extensive change bring growth in some areas of the economy and deprivation in others. To an individual, the results of massive change can create opportunities for growth and excitement but this is often associated with a tiring and deprivation of both the flesh and the spirit. It affects us all differently and this may account for the confusion in terminology and understanding of the word stress. Excess pressure or stress is very definitely present in the 21st Century - a fact of life.

# Body Reactions

As stress managers, our experience indicates many clients are unaware of the indications of stress. It is therefore an important part of this book to raise awareness of the signals of stress to help as many people as possible develop early recognition and take preventative action.

The indications of stress are many and varied but all are the result of a response to a challenge of some sort.

## Challenge – what is it?

Every day, in the workplace and at home, we face questions, difficulties, problems, situations and options on simple and complex issues. Such challenges require us to make decisions, which can be straightforward or difficult. We all react very differently to questions and situations; some feel offended by a question that others would find amusing. There are therefore varying perceptions of the same experience.

When a person experiences a challenge they initially react in the way all human bodies have responded since the Stone Age:
  • extra adrenaline (epinephrine) is produced
  • other neurotransmitters and hormones are produced
  • the heart rate increases

17

- the breathing rate increases
- blood pressure increases
- muscles become tense
- body hairs become erect
- pupils of the eye dilate
- sweat is produced
- may need to go to the toilet

This is an instant, natural reaction and serves the purpose of alerting the body. It is known as the 'fight or flight' reaction – preparing the body to fight or run away. It occurs with every challenge we experience – an unpleasant phone call from a customer, a large domestic bill we are unable to pay, being shouted at or just feeling uncomfortable in a dimly lit street on the way home after working late.

One person's challenge is another person's nightmare

In the scenario at the beginning of the chapter, Debbie and James returned home to find their house burgled. They would be instantly in an alert state. What if the burglar was still there? What horrors were they going to find?

In technical terms, the body courses with many chemicals (including adrenaline). These are quickly absorbed back into the body when we physically fight or run away.

Debbie and James reacted differently (as men and women often do). James stormed into the house making lots of noise and throwing open doors and shouting; Debbie held back with her hand over her mouth, fighting back the tears and saying "Oh no! Oh no!". Within minutes, both had assessed the situation and slid into coping mode – phoning the police, checking what was missing and tidying up. Debbie didn't sleep well but James slept soundly and both felt a little disturbed the following morning.

In body terms, a balanced state was restored. Visual and emotional memories had been created or re-stimulated but on the surface, both were coping well.

Many of the challenges we face result in an emotional response, rather than a physical fight or tactical retreat. We become annoyed, angry, irritated or embarrassed and though we may wish to hit someone or run away it is not socially appropriate, especially if we want to keep our job or stay on the right side of the law. If the 'fight or flight' reaction is repeated regularly throughout the day, and we do not fight or run away, it has the effect of making the body feel drained and tense and the mind exhausted.

Some people react more intensely to challenges than others and the pace of recovery to their state of balanced well-being is slower. If the challenges keep occurring, their body and mind balance is not restored sufficiently and the result is ill health to some degree - stress.

# The attitude to stress

If you break your leg because too much pressure has been exerted on the bones you can expect lots of sympathy and understanding. Depending on the circumstances, you may have to take some ribbing but in general you'll be given time off work and arrangements will be made to make your life amenable. However, if instead of a physical difficulty your normally effective mental state becomes reduced through excess pressure you may not be afforded the same understanding.

> Every person is unique and may react differently

Why is it that we differentiate in such a way between physical and mental conditions? Physical ill health is OK, acceptable and non-threatening, whereas mental is scary, uncontrollable and weird. It is OK to be off work with a cold but not insomnia symptoms. It's serious, but OK, to have high blood pressure or a heart attack but not as acceptable to develop panic attacks or anxiety. This is a cultural belief that we need to address.

In the board rooms of companies there is still discussion about the presence or absence of stress in the workplace. For some, admitting that staff are under excessive pressure is indicative of an instability or weakness in the employees or the management. For others, it is an indication that staff are being put under too much pressure and decisions need to be made about how to get the work done without damaging their health.

To a busy lawyer, stress could be too many cases over a prolonged period of time and not enough time to prepare and research. To a casualty nurse it may be shift work, paperwork and lack of available beds to cope with increasing numbers of patients. To a fireman it may not be fire-fighting itself, but the sitting around for much of a shift, waiting for a call out. To an office manager, stress could be incessant change over a period of time from a rapidly developing company. To Debbie and James, both active in the workplace, it was the added distress of a home burglary.

Accepting that stress is a reality can be a challenge in itself for some people who like to infer that all pressures are just part of life and those who succumb are inferior beings.

Try stretching a rubber band – it is very pliable and accommodating but if you stretch it too far, it will break. This is an excellent analogy with a human being – stretch or push them too far and they will break!

# Stress warnings

The body is an amazing machine but it has finite tolerance levels just like an elastic band.

It is impossible to avoid challenge or pressure in daily life and complete absence of it is achieved only in death. We humans need a reason to get up in the morning, and regular challenge to keep us motivated. This results in an active interest in life, work and the environment around them. The person who has lost their interest in living doesn't respond to a challenge and sees it as a depressing mountain of difficult routes and impossible climbs. This makes them an ineffective employee and a difficult person to live with.

Excessive pressures on individuals makes them imbalanced and they begin to show symptoms of ill health. This is a slow build up and can take weeks, months or years. There is a middle stage of adaptation where the body begins to adapt to the physiological changes and pressures being experienced and it attempts to restore 'normality'. The final stage of too much pressure (which is not always reached), is burn out or breakdown.

The effects of stress for the individual are personal and varied. Identifying the symptoms can be difficult as they often start small and become more serious. Sustained pressure will lead to a combination of some the reactions shown below. These are a warning that health is being adversely affected. The reactions have been listed in three categories and the lists are not exhaustive.

## Check out your stress symptoms

| Emotional | Behavioural | Health |
|---|---|---|
| Aggression | Absent from work | Absence of |
| Anger | Accident prone | periods – not due |
| Anxiety | Avoidance of social | to pregnancy |
| Apathy | interaction | Aches and pains – |
| Boredom | Constant clock watching | notably in chest and |
| Confusion | Constant worrying | back |
| Crying without | Cynicism | Breathing difficulties |
| apparent reason | Excessive eating | Diarrhoea attacks |
| Depression | Excessive use of | Dizziness & nausea |
| Discouragement | alcohol/stimulants | Dryness of mouth |
| Fatigue | Family/relationship | Fatigue at work/home |
| Frustration | conflict | Frequent colds/flu |
| Guilt | Forgetfulness | Headaches/migraine |
| Irritability | General emotional | Frequent urination |
| Low self esteem | outbursts | Insomnia |
| Moodiness | Impulsive patterns of | Increased heart rate/ |
| Negative thoughts | behaviour | blood pressure |
| Nervousness | Inappropriate laughter | Loss of sex drive |
| Paranoia | Lack of concentration | Numbness in limbs |
| Resentment | Loss of appetite | Skin complaints |
| Sadness without | Preoccupation with self | Sleeping difficulties |
| reason | Restlessness | Sweating |
| Sense of failure | Speech difficulties | Hot & cold flushes |
| Sense of helplessness | Strong resistance to | |
| Sense of isolation | change | |
| Sense of shame | Procrastination | |

How many of these reactions can you honestly tick?

How many would your partner or work colleague tick if **they** were assessing you?

# Stress awareness    date_____

Make a list of any of the above reactions you are currently
experiencing and quantify them on a scale of 1 - 5:

where 1 is occasionally
        3 is regularly
        5 is very often.
Date it so you can compare with a future assessment.

|            | reaction | grade (1 – 5) |
|------------|----------|---------------|
| e.g        | *insomnia* | 4 |
|            | ........................................................................... | |
|            | ........................................................................... | |
|            | ........................................................................... | |
|            | ........................................................................... | |
|            | ........................................................................... | |

This is the start of your awareness of reactions to excess
pressure.

# Stressed or Busy?

In the workplace, on the street and at home, it is common to overhear someone saying "I'm so stressed!" or "this makes me so stressed!". However they may well not be showing any of the above indicators. A description which is more appropriate of how they feel is 'busy'.

Busy feels as if we have lots to do - we look and feel involved, motivated and enthusiastic. The result of being busy can induce tiredness which is a natural reaction. If the tiredness has been caused by mental effort then exercise will stimulate the parts the mind could not reach. Sleep can revive and refresh a tired body and mind.

Many people today seem to have forgotten to allow themselves to feel satisfied with a good day's work. Knowing that you have completed a satisfactory level of
activity and achieved what you set out to do (or more often, reacted well to the unexpected) is satisfying and encouraging. If this is followed by a relaxed pace at home, a balance of acceptable pressure can be achieved. If, however, home is as frantic as work, the pressure just continues and eventually stress reactions will appear.

The reactions attributable to excess pressure are caused by regular body responses and the following Stress Gremlin model has been developed as a result of working with and observing a large number of different and varied people during our many thousands of consultations. Clients find it satisfactorily explains the way they feel at various points in their life.

> Knowledge of stress will help you deal with it

24

# Stress Gremlins©

## 'everyone can become stressed'

Stress gremlins reside in everyone – especially in the body system that is sensitive to excess pressure.

Where do you feel pain or discomfort when you are experiencing excess pressure – stomach? head? spine? muscles?

As you read through this book you will develop more awareness of your own pressure points and begin to listen to them. Knowing yourself and your particular signs may help you to start positive preventative measures.

We all have gremlins……………they are part of life.

Stress gremlins thrive and feed on worry and fear (real or imagined), guilt, low self-esteem, resentment, jealousy and other strong emotions They are soothed, calmed and reduced by happiness, joy and pleasure. Depending on which emotions are dominant in your life, the balance can change from well-being to ill health.

The gremlins can settle in areas of the body that are sensitive to stress:

- in the nervous system the result could be headaches or migraines
- in the muscular system you could develop inflammation in your muscles and tendons, producing pain and discomfort
- in the skeletal system it could affect joints, possibly resulting in arthritis or similar inflammatory conditions
- In the liver, stress could reduce its ability to handle toxins or affect one of the many other functions of this vital organ

How often do you feed your stress gremlins?

What emotions do you feed them?

# Causes of personal stress

We have already established that stress is a build-up of pressures. These can be external (from people or situations) as well as internal (personal thoughts and feelings). What is exciting and motivating for 'James' could create fear and trepidation for 'Debbie'. Stress depends on the number and severity of challenges we experience and react to. Some challenges can result in stress and are called **stressors.**

> Stress depends on the number and severity of challenges we experience and react negatively to

## External stressors

Serious life events can result in stress reactions and some of these are listed below. Recent experience and research has shown that it is not the individual life events but the number of them you are exposed to at any one time which saps your emotional strength and feeds your stress gremlins.

## Life events

Death of a life partner
Divorce
Separation
Death of a family member
An addition to the family
Personal injury or illness
Marriage
Bullying / harassment
Redeployment
Redundancy
Moving home
A court case / jail sentence
Financial crisis
Extended families
Becoming a step parent/child

Coping with a disability
Retirement

Tick any of the above which have affected you in recent months and add any others of your own, remembering that if it is causing **you** worry and distress then it is important to **you** (ignore what others say – the first step in self awareness is acknowledgement of how **you** are affected)

............................................................................

............................................................................

............................................................................

When coping with one of the above life events you experience many emotions, some of which feed you gremlins and for a while this can reduce the effectiveness of your immune system and your natural energy field.

As time passes and solutions are developed body and mind can be restored to the state which is acceptable for you and your gremlins relax. If you are dealing with more than one life event or personal crisis the body systems are more severely effected and it takes (your gremlins) longer to recover.

This gremlin model has proved acceptable and even attractive to clients as it helps them to take control of feeding their gremlins or experience the result!

## Case Study

'Mark' had a new job which he was finding enjoyable. His new colleagues were friendly and encouraging but there were a few new concepts he had to learn. He had just started a course to learn the work and was finding it quite difficult but stimulating.

Since his father died he had a close relationship with his mother who had been ill for some months. He visited her regularly in a hospital which was some distance away and the visit took up a whole evening. He seemed to be coping well and his family were supportive but he missed a parents' evening and concert at his daughter's school and she was extremely upset.

Over the next few weeks he became withdrawn and irritable, snapping at both family and colleagues. He began to get pains in his chest and experienced his first panic attack. He was still visiting the hospital to see his mother, but had missed a few days of the course and was falling behind. He became uncommunicative and his relationships began to suffer. He went to the doctor and was diagnosed with stress.

This case study shows how work and personal life are intimately intertwined. 'Mark' could probably have dealt with either one of the life events (new job / mother's illness), but both together became too much. In future chapters we will explore current methods of treatment for the diagnosis of stress which Mark was given.

## Internal stressors

Sometimes, people are excellent at pulling their own strings and inducing stress. A good example of this is worry.

## Worry

People who worry a lot, work themselves up into a great state. You may be one of these people, and if not, I'm sure you've got one in your family or a close friend. Their language is peppered with "what if?" and they are past masters at creating scenarios that never happen. While doing this, their body is in a state of alertness and readiness - a state of concern, anxiety and apprehension. This is excellent food for stress gremlins.

## Internal dialogue

Another internal activity we do, is talk to ourselves. Sometimes the chatter inside your head is fascinating as your mind discusses the pro and cons of a situation.

Most people will recognise the above scenario. When you are listening, there are many thoughts buzzing around your head. You may be rehearsing how you are going to respond when your colleague finishes talking, asking yourself if your answer or attitude is congruent, questioning your and their motives, encouraging or discouraging yourself. It can take a lot of practise to listen intently and remove the internal chatter of the brain.

---

**Case Study**

'Sarah' was listening to 'Jane' telling her about a meeting she had attended. 'Sarah' was nodding and showing interest but was also thinking about the homeward journey that evening. When she had come into work in the morning the trains had all been late and very crowded. She had heard at lunch time that there was still a problem with the trains and she had to get to the child minder before 5 o'clock. She also had some office e-mails to deal with and was trying to remember how many. 'Jane' finished her story and they began to plan how to incorporate what Jane had learned into their working practices. 'Sarah' realised she had no idea what the main points of 'Jane's' comments were.................

---

Start to notice when you worry

At other times the internal dialogue is negative and unhelpful as you tell yourself you will never be able to do something. This is based on our belief systems which in turn are based on our early life experiences. People who have been told they are clumsy / unable to swim / hopeless at maths etc find themselves repeating this mantra regularly throughout their life and it becomes a fulfilling prophesy. This concept is developed further in Chapter 2.

# Perfection

This is another powerful internal stressor. Perfectionists strive for faultlessness but they can always see a slight imperfection that needs to be modified. They often have problems with dead lines because they never reach the perfect result. This can make them difficult to work with. They seldom reach the desired outcome and move on with a sense of failure, despite being told their work / product / result is totally acceptable.

The opposite of a perfectionist is a **speedy** person. This type cuts corners and enjoys completing tasks and moving on to the next. They are often irritated by slow, pedantic perfectionists who can build up their stress level.

Prevention is better than cure in relation to stress, so it follows that awareness helps to flag up a situation that needs to be managed before it gets out of hand. The best person to deal with your stress is YOU. Individuals are responsible for how they think, react and behave in the situations they create or find themselves in. A good way to begin, is to assess the risk of being affected by stress. To make a valuable assessment of risk you need to know which factors of life affect and upset you. You also need to be aware of what helps you to cope.

It is therefore important to take a complete, all round (holistic) view of the causes and indicators of your stress. Stand back and assess:

- how you feel at present
- what events are currently challenging
- are you predominantly negative or positive in outlook
- who is pulling your strings
- how you are currently coping

> No one achieves perfection- settle for your best

- on a scale of 1 – 5 where is your stress level (1 = low; 5 = high)
- is this stress level acceptable at present

Often the outcome of an assessment is encouraging and you realise you are not stressed yet. This is the good time to assess the strategies you are currently using which work

By making such an assessment you are taking control of your personal situation. Throughout the book we will encourage you to make regular personal assessments and develop your awareness of the best coping strategies for you.

# Chapter
# 2

# Awareness of ourselves

- signs of stress

- individual diagnostic systems

- emotional challenges

- positive and negative states

- beliefs

- supporting beliefs

==

"You look really pale and drawn today" James said to Debbie as he was about to leave for a work meeting. "No, I'm OK" said Debbie and turned away to stack the dishwasher after their rushed breakfast. She planned to do a quick shop before going to the Post Office where she worked part time. When she arrived at the supermarket she was a bit short of time as there had been a big hold-up on the road due to some road works. Everything had been moved around since she was last there and she had to ask staff where the washing powders had gone as she was running out of time. She began to feel breathless and when she was waiting at the checkout she felt everyone must be able to hear her heart beat and it felt as if it would explode out of her chest any minute. She felt tight in the chest and fleetingly wondered if she was having a heart attack. Debbie pushed her trolley aside and sidled past the waiting shoppers.

"Pushing in like that" one woman said but Debbie kept going as she felt she had to get outside. In the car park, she leant against a barrier and tried to slow her breathing down but that felt impossible. Someone came over to her and asked if she was alright. Debbie could hardly speak and the woman's hand on her arm felt like a vice grip. Eventually her breathing got better and she returned to the car. "I feel such a fool" she said to herself. "What will James say?" she thought. She began to feel slightly better and decided to drive home carefully. She called the Post Office to tell them she was unwell and decided to sit down for an hour or two. She was beginning to feel better and soon was up and about preparing the evening meal for James and Jonathan, their son.

==========================================

What had brought on Debbie's 'turn'? Was it something she had eaten? Was it an indication that she had high blood pressure or a developing heart problem? Was it a nagging worry that was eating away at her and making her nervous? Was it just that she had been rushing about?

One of the best ways to tackle your stress is to develop an awareness of how your body reacts to excess pressures. Find out what feeds your gremlins and make some plans to reduce their food!

Many of the following concepts and exercises are used not only to work with stress but are helpful for all aspects of life and developing well-being.

Stress is the result of a build up of lots of mind and body reactions to challenges we are faced with. It is not just **one** challenge it is one **several times over** or **several challenges at the same time**. This has the effect of feeding the gremlins which will eventually become active, upsetting your body systems. The build-up time may be over a period of weeks, months or years, it doesn't matter. If you place a few grains of sand in a bowl every day, eventually they will fill the bowl. A worry or problem may last for many years, and the body adapts as long as possible, but eventually it could 'spring a leak' or 'blow a gasket' …………….choose your own metaphor!

# Signs of Stress

It is my experience that most people have a diagnostic system – a part of your body that always goes wrong when you are under pressure. This is an indication that one of your systems is less effective that the others and this is where health problems appear.

For instance, if you:

- are asthmatic
- experience skin problems like eczema, psoriasis or dermatitis
- have high blood pressure
- suffer from angina or other heart conditions
- experience digestive upsets (IBS, Colitis )
- are very nervous and easily upset

Recognise which part of your body reacts to the stress response

one or more of these conditions will often get worse when you are seriously challenged or concerned by work or a family problem.

Debbie's panic attack was an indication that her system is upset – possibly by the way she feels about the burglary.

# Individual Diagnostic Systems
## (the gremlins at work)

Now think very carefully…when you are upset by something or someone, how does it make you feel? What part of your body tells you it is distressed?

| | |
|---|---|
| Do you get stomach cramps or 'butterflies' in your abdomen | YES/NO |
| Do you experience acid reflux? | YES/NO |
| Do you need to release the contents of your bowels? | YES/NO |
| Do you feel sick? | YES/NO |
| Do the muscles around your neck and shoulders become tight and tense? | YES/NO |
| Do you get pains in any of your joints? | YES/NO |
| Do you suffer from headaches or migraines? | YES/NO |
| Do you seem to produce endless streams of urine? | YES/NO |
| Do you feel pain in your back? | YES/NO |
| Please add your own symptoms: | |

...................................................................................

...................................................................................

This helps you see where your gremlins reside:

Draw a gremlin or two in the area(s) where
stress affects YOU.

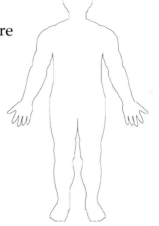

Recognise your
body's messages

Stress is very personal and where it affects you varies from
person to person.

In the same way, how we react to pressure depends on our
personal biological system. DNA profiling has shown that
unless you are an identical twin no one else has the same
profile. Siblings are similar but differences are recognisable. Our
DNA dictates how our systems function and there are many
minor variations. which is one of the reasons we may react
differently to drugs, treatments and stress.

By identifying how your body reacts to pressure you will begin
self-awareness. Most of us know when we are being challenged
and how we react but we are sometimes very good at ignoring
it.

Some people just accept they suffer from headaches, stomach
upsets or panic attacks, without questioning what their body is
telling them. Such symptoms are a message from your body
that you need to review the situation.

Good questions to ask would be:

- "What is this headache/stomach ache/back ache about?"
- "What is currently upsetting me?

40

• "What, if anything, can I do about it?"

---

**Case Study**

**Part one**

'Alison' had been asked to do a presentation to her senior manager and her colleagues about a new project she was involved in. It was the first time she had been asked to do anything like this and she was very worried.

Within a few days she was suffering from headaches and her eye began to twitch.

---

Until 'Alison' was asked to do the presentation, she had no symptoms but did occasionally get headaches. She had never had an eye problem before.
Her nervous system is her diagnostic system

What was currently upsetting 'Alison'?
• the forthcoming presentation.

What can she do about it?
• accept that she finds this a challenge
• be aware that this is a short-term challenge and will soon be over
• take advice on how her company usually do presentations
• remember that she knows more about this project than anyone else (this is why she has been asked to do the presentation)
• practice giving her presentation in front of a mirror
• use cards with headings to keep her on track

- learn deep abdominal breathing to help to calm her nerves
- visualise giving the presentation successfully

---

**Case study**

**Part two**

'Alison' took on board the above plan and very soon her symptoms subsided. A colleague helped her with the technicalities of Power Point and soon she had an excellent aid to help her present her project. She practised what she wanted to say and her confidence developed.

The presentation went well and she was commended for her fluency and progress with the project.

---

From this experience, 'Alison' learned to recognise indicators from her nervous system and tried to control the causes as much as possible.

# Emotional challenges

Sometimes we can recognise symptoms of distress but are unable to identify an obvious reason. No matter how hard you search, you are unable to find a plausible reason for your stress indicators. In such circumstances, the causes are often to be found in subconscious emotional thoughts.

Emotions are mental associations that are triggered by experiences. They can be controlled but are often suppressed.

The mind reacts to subconscious thoughts and sometimes we have no idea where the emotion has come from.

When emotional stimulation occurs regularly, an imbalance will occur in the organ or system and eventually a symptom will appear. It could be a problem with a kidney, the liver, the skin or any other organ.

A great start to reducing stress reactions, is recognising that an emotion is the cause of how you feel or how you are reacting. This does not mean you need to be self analysing all the time. That would be an obsessive over reaction. A quiet awareness that emotions can be extremely powerful within the body is enough. Some calming deep abdominal breathing is helpful to still a fluttering heart beat. If you don't want to be calm and it is appropriate, let the emotion out.

recognise that a build up of emotions can lead to stress

# Positive and Negative states

When you feel negative and low, your body is de-energised, This can be demonstrated very clearly in the following exercise:

---

## You need a friend to help for this activity

Stand with your feet slightly apart and raise you right or left arm until it is at right angles to your body.
Think of someone you love and a great experience you had with them.
Ask your friend to push down on your arm while you resist.
Note the effect.
Now think of an unpleasant experience you had and feel it, see it, remember how it sounded.
Ask you friend to repeat the arm pressure while you try to resist and note the change.

The difference is usually dramatic.
When thinking positively it is easy to resist –
When thinking negatively it is hard to resist the same pressure and your arm is pushed down easily.

---

Testing muscles in this way is used by Kinesiologists. Kinesiology is a relatively recent therapeutic practice that uses muscle testing to demonstrate positive and negative body states very accurately and effectively. It is a holistic approach, detecting the whole body's response to carefully composed questions.

You do not even need to be tested, to be aware of your whole body feelings. You know what it feels like to be in a positive or a negative state. The above visualisation of a positive state demonstrates how much we are able to influence our body states. Sport psychologists at the top levels, have encouraged their athletes to access a positive, winning state. When a positive state is combined with appropriate physical training and a desire to win, it often results in a successful challenge to an established record.

> check your attitude regularly – is it positive or negative?

# What are YOUR beliefs and values?

Every moment of every day, our brain is processing information and this is influenced by our belief system. Our beliefs originate from all our life experiences and are based on our core values.

Circle which of the following values/beliefs are important to you:

| | | | |
|---|---|---|---|
| ability | accountable | ambition | choice |
| commitment | competitiveness | completion | congruence |
| control | courage | determination | efficiency |
| good health | honesty | integrity | patience |
| perfection | persistence | politeness | preparedness |
| privacy | reliability | thoughtfulness | |

others...................................................................................

To rank them in order may be rather difficult, but if you can, it clarifies your perspectives even more. Are there any patterns amongst the words you have chosen? These will be in line with your profiles in Chapter 3.

Some of the above values are very demanding – they add a lot of pressure to life and for some this is essential; for others, it is a burden.

## Case Study

'Alan' was a perfectionist. He was proud to be a perfectionist. His home was immaculate, his grass and garden was perfect. He worked diligently as a credit controller for a medium sized company and his work was always up to date. His colleagues found him 'picky' as he like everything absolutely correct. His neighbours admired his garden but none tried to emulate him.

He had an accident and broke his leg in two places which meant he was unable to be active. His wife was unable to keep everything in its pristine condition and soon they began to argue as he became irritable. He began to have anxiety and panic attacks which occurred both at home and work.

After an assessment in our centre, he realised his perfectionism was the cause of his anxiety. He found it difficult to change his outlook but his desire to be well again overcame a habit he had held for a very long time.

No doubt. 'Alan's' anxiety would have reduced when his broken leg mended and he was able to regain control of his home and work commitments, but in the meantime he found some other interesting hobbies and realised how much time his perfectionist behaviour had taken up, to the exclusion of other activities.

Not everyone has the same principles and values. Disagreement and distrust can result when there is uncertainty and lack of awareness of another person's principles. Many of the above values and principles work well for people and help them achieve their goals and aims in life but sometimes these values can also be limiting and restricting. It requires a degree of tolerance to appreciate different outlooks and perspectives but it is well worth the effort to achieve understanding of others and an understanding of yourself.

> Get to know your core values and what is really important to you

## Beliefs and challenging language

Listening to conversations is a fascinating experience! Some people pepper their sentences with words like 'should', 'must', 'ought' and 'have to'.

For example:
"I really feel I have to attend this meeting" ………..you can hear the reluctance in this sentence and probably also see it in the person's face as the words are uttered.
"I should go to the gym more often but I just never seem to have the time" ….. how often do we know what is good for us but always find an excuse?

These words –**should, must, have to and ought** - are very demanding, creating guilt, anxiety or personal pressure. They suggest that the individual has no choice or control over the situation. They indicate that the person is limited to options from outside influences. While this may be partly true – we always have a choice. The choice may seem unrealistic but when you realise that you do have a choice, it is surprising how it seems to move the goalposts.

The choice can be recognised by changing the coercive words:

Try changing 'should'
           'must'                             to 'could'
           'ought'
           'have to'

'Could' means you have a choice – it may not be a big choice but you do have one and this enables you to search for other alternatives.

Sometimes, social pressures mean that doing what **we** want would damage an important relationship or would not be appropriate but at least when you realise you are choosing to keep the status quo, you are making a choice and are therefore more in control.

**Case Study**

'George' was a successful accountant who had worked for a large company that had recently been taken over by an even larger PLC. Slowly but surely he came to realise that the new ethos was at odds with his outlook and he decided to set up on his own. After a few years he had a thriving business and worked with 5 other colleagues. He found he was working long hours and it was affecting his family life. He regularly made comments like " I should leave early but there is always so much to do" and "I probably should get another accountant but a recession is forecast".

We discussed how these thoughts and feelings were very coercive and left him feeling inadequate and ineffective. We then changed the sentences to:

"I *could* leave early"...............and "I *could* get another accountant"

This changed the sentences completely. Suddenly, he had a choice! He could leave early but currently chose not to. The reason for not leaving early was then discussed and he agreed to leave work at 5 pm (not early, just on time) one day a week. This worked and helped him to be slightly more involved in his family commitments. As far as the other statement was concerned he looked at the options and then brainstormed some more, resulting in the acquisition of a part time accountant who wanted a few hours a week to keep her skills up to date while taking time out for her family.

## Try this exercise:

Write down some 'shoulds', 'musts', 'ought to' or 'have to'.....

I should ..........................................................................

I must ............................................................................

I have to .........................................................................

I ought to ........................................................................

I should ..........................................................................

I must ............................................................................

I have to .........................................................................

I ought to ........................................................................

I need to .........................................................................

I should ..........................................................................

Once you have completed as many as you can, ask your self – whose 'should' etc are they? Who says you should do these things?

If the answer is 'me' you seem to be coercing yourself to do a lot of things.

If the answer is other people, it is good to be aware of the demands that other people are putting on you. It doesn't mean you have to change but it is good to be aware of who is pulling your strings.

> change 'should' to 'could' as often as possible

Now change all the coercive words to 'could'. Actively score out 'should', 'have to', 'ought' and 'must' and replace it with 'could'. Now you have a choice!
You could do these things that are pressures in your life, but what would happen if you didn't?

If you decide you still want to do them, do them with conviction and joy in your heart. This will create a positive state instead of the negative state, which would have resulted from coercion.

It is always good to induce the 'feel good' factor and you will notice a change in reaction from the receiver of your action. It is a win/win occasion! When you have chosen to do something with positive intent, this is recognised at an emotional and cellular level in our body and results in a very successful outcome.

## Limiting Beliefs

You are now aware of some words that have been forcing you to do things and may or may not choose to change the pattern. We also have many beliefs which are rooted in our childhood experiences and which we use and repeat regularly.

In the first few years of life, a baby is dependant for sustenance and security from adults. Very soon she begins to exert her own influence on adults. Like a sponge she absorbs attitudes and responds to feelings creating a learning response that will be repeated if the result is good. She learns quickly what pleases and what does not. She learns how to please and what gets her what she wants.

Interactions like these help to confirm a set of beliefs, which will not change, even if there are very good reasons why they should. As the child grows up, more and more people begin to influence her life. Parents are the initial influencers but grandparents, other siblings and adults in the family add their influence. If she goes to a nursery, the carer or carers will also affect her belief patterns, as the first three to five years are extremely significant in the development of a person's belief patterns. Teachers, peers and other significant adults can also have a strong influence. This is a huge subject and has been the topic of many academic papers, books and symposia and is still the subject of learned and often heated discussion.

However, basic observation and awareness of family, friends and colleagues shows us that we have firmly held belief patterns based on early life. You can hear this in our language and explanations of why we react and respond the way we do.

To a child, a comment overheard or personally directed can sometimes create a response which is unintentional or completely out of proportion. You know the sort of thing – a tired parent snaps at a child saying "you are so clumsy" and a belief pattern can be set for life. The child will accept the statement and may even repeat it or expect to be clumsy and then usually manages to live up to the expectation.

Similar statements are often heard relating to body shape / weight. A brother who teases his sister that she is fat, may repeat this mantra many times, especially when he sees it annoys or upsets her. A belief pattern is set up in her mind that she is fat – which she may or may not be – but even when she has developed into a svelte young woman, she still may believe she is fat. This does not occur in every individual but susceptible people often hold beliefs that are totally inappropriate and they are unaware of this fact.

Many people have a belief that they can't do maths. Numeracy seems to be a great challenge for many in our society. Parents often share their beliefs with their children by saying "I was never any good at maths at school', suggesting it is some sort of inherited trait. This may allow a son who is currently struggling with the intricacies of subtraction, multiplication, division or algebra, to stack up his belief that he is unable to do maths. A self-fulfilling prophesy is then set up for even the most basic tasks with numbers.

> If you think you can't do it you won't!

Such limiting beliefs restrict our expectations, not only in maths but in many varied areas of life. If people can become aware of the way they restrict their options it becomes the start of new opportunities and possibilities. It all depends on the individual's personality and outlook on life whether opportunities are seen as exciting or scary, enabling or worrying.

# What are your limiting beliefs?

Over the next few days, listen to yourself as you converse with friends, colleagues and family and notice any limiting statements you make regularly.

Some examples could be:

"I am a lazy person"

"I can't face it

"I am useless at physics"

"It's too difficult"

"I can't be bothered"

"I can't get out of the rut"

"Always the bridesmaid, never the bride"

"I don't know which way to turn"

"It always happens to me"

"I'm always last/second

"There's nothing I can do"

"I'm too old/young"

"I've never been lucky"

"I'm clumsy"

"I can't change, I had a bad childhood"

How might these statements affect what you do and what you want to do?

If you changed the statement(s) to it's positive equivalent, how would that change your options?

Limiting beliefs restrict individuals and keep them in their comfort zones. In principle there is nothing wrong with being in a comfort zone but sometimes it has the effect of limiting our options when we need or want to expand our horizons.

---

**Case Study**

'Geraldine' believed she lacked confidence. She had a 'first' from Oxford and a great job but didn't have a boyfriend because she had no confidence when it came to dates.

In further discussion she admitted to being a very private person and believed that she could not share her personal life with anyone else. Geraldine recounted how her father had often commented that personal and public life should be separated and it was important to "keep yourself to yourself".

She had abided by this principle and now seemed to find it difficult to share any part of her life. She had limited friendships at work and her hobbies were rather solitary. The result was a severe lack of confidence.

Geraldine worked at developing her confidence through psychotherapy and neuro linguistic programming (NLP) and both her work and social life improved.

---

'Geraldine' and others have changed their life by becoming aware of their limiting beliefs and deciding they were no longer applicable. This released their fetters and allowed them to explore new options which were exciting, scary and challenging. When people realise they have many more options than they thought by releasing their limiting beliefs, their world becomes stimulating and so do they.

become aware of your self-limiting language

## Changing an unhelpful belief

There are many ways to change an unhelpful belief and many self help books to aid in the process as well as professional help from stress managers and psychotherapists. It does not take long to change a belief if you have thought through carefully the reasons for changing and what would be a more appropriate belief.

Identify a belief that is holding you back (see above) and acting as a stressor
(I am...too young / old / fat / thin / rich / poor / unworthy / useless / hopeless....)

Ask yourself –   who told you that?
                what evidence is there of this belief?
                why do I believe it?
                who tries to encourage me to believe
                otherwise?
                what is their agenda?
                do I really want to change this belief?
                who else will it affect?
                am I ready to change now?

/hen you are satisfied with these answers and have
 decided to let go of your unhelpful belief, tell someone
 you trust.
 decide when you are going to make the change
 decide how you are going to make the change do it

# Making the change

When was the last time you weighed up the pros and cons and decided that A was better than B and changed your opinion? This is a process we all take part in regularly and is based on an emotional reaction that change is necessary. When politicians change their mind and make policy changes there is a great amount of comment relating to 'about turn'. The most well documented comment about not changing was Margaret Thatcher's well publicised comment "the lady is not for turning". This was said with great confidence and not a little haughtiness and was no doubt the decision after much thought but it closed a door to any possible change in attitude.

Change is what life is about. There are many changes, some large, some small and they affect everyone. However not everyone chooses to be affected and prefers to ignore change or take it very slowly – and that is fine. Other people jump on every option for change and love the variety and the buzz – and that is fine also.

Making a change of an unhelpful belief which is limiting your progress or your life may seem dramatic. The results can also be dramatic as you release yourself from the chains of limitation and open up new perspectives and horizons.

# 'Breaking the disc' of your belief

Since you may have been telling yourself for years that you were unable to do something it is exciting to start to believe that you will be able to do it. You can start by challenging the belief statement every time you hear yourself stating it. Remind yourself that you have decided to stop repeating your unhelpful belief and encourage your self not to say it. Soon your subconscious mind will react like a laser beam on a disc that has been scratched or damaged and miss that part out.

Now is the time to replace the disc with your new belief. Regularly repeat your new belief to yourself and put plans in place to help it to become a reality. If you want to be better at maths, join a class that is appropriate for your current ability and will raise your standards. With your new belief that you can do maths you will pass the necessary exams after adequate study.

You will notice that your required result will not instantly happen, but it will soon or eventually happen because you have opened the door, which was definitely shut, to allow development and progress.

'Breaking the disc' is one method of installing change. Others methods incorporate hypnotherapy, visualisation, pro active counselling, neuro linguistic programming (NLP), and cognitive behavioural therapy. There are many books on these subjects and trained practitioners if help is required.

# Supporting Beliefs

Supporting beliefs are the opposite of limiting beliefs. They nurture and encourage self-esteem. They provide a firm base on which to support a fulfilled life. They reduce stress by enhancing self-esteem and self-belief. It helps if the supporting belief is regularly enhanced from experience and observation.

In 2003 Michael Watson, the boxer, completed the London marathon. After his fight with Chris Eubank in 1991 he was diagnosed with severe brain damage and was told by his neurosurgeon that he would never walk or even talk again.

Deep in his heart and psyche he did not believe this and decided that he was going to challenge all the negative expectations in a very dynamic way – by attempting the most prestigious race in Britain. Slowly but very surely he dictated his progress, often against the beliefs of his medical team and recovered his faculties beyond everyone's expectations except his own. This example will undoubtedly encourage many invalids in the future and is an outstanding example of the power of positive self-belief.

> Believe you can and you will

If a world-class athlete does not believe she can be the best then she will never **try** to achieve the ultimate award.

---

## What are your supporting beliefs?

Some examples could be:

I am good at swimming, football, riding, running, walking etc
I had/have loving, nurturing parents.
I have a strong faith.
I know where I am going.

...................................................................

...................................................................

...................................................................

---

Supporting beliefs are nurtured deep within the body and mind creating energy, commitment and enthusiasm to achieve a chosen goal.

# Chapter 3

# What kind of person am I?

- lifestyle

- personality

*"the life which is unexamined is not worth living"*
*Plato*

===

James was sitting at his office desk, trying to focus on his new role in the recently merged company. He was lucky to have kept a job, as many of his former colleagues had been made redundant. This new role was different and involved more networking and customer facing. When he had the interview he felt is would be a good challenge and shake his ideas up a bit. He felt he had been getting a bit set in his ways before the merger but some of the new people seemed very switched on and he would need to get his act together soon.

It was early afternoon and the sun was streaming through the window as he stretched back in his chair and yawned. "I always seem to be tired these days" he commented to his colleague "so much to do I never know where to start". The phone rang, startling him, and he heard his new line manager's clipped tones asking where the report was on the meeting they had been to yesterday. "We need the key points urgently, so we can plan the campaign" he said. "I am just doing them now" James mumbled, "I'll e mail them to you shortly". With a sigh, he picked up the mouse and began to work.

===============================================

# Lifestyle

How we spend every 24 hours in a day is sometimes by design but often by default. The quality of various activities and the value we put on them can act as a stressor or a reliever. James' new work is challenging and demanding which is sapping his energy and he takes little opportunity to revitalise himself. It is good to assess your lifestyle fairly regularly, especially if you are experiencing a lot of change.

## Lifestyle Awareness and Evaluation

The following questionnaire researches lifestyle facts and personal awareness.

The facts can be scored and questions relating to facts are marked with an ✳

Awareness questions are for your understanding and perception and are not scored.

Score each ✻ question 1 – 5
(where 1 = almost always/yes and 5 = never/no)

How many hours do you normally sleep

............

✻ I get sufficient sleep for my needs

............

If not how many hours sleep would you ideally have every 24 hours

............

✻ I eat regular meals

............

✻ I eat junk food/prepared convenience meals very occasionally

............

✻ I eat lots of fresh fruit and vegetables +/- meat/fish/poultry

............

✻ I am the appropriate weight for my height

............

✻ I drink 2 litres of water each day

............

✻ I do not smoke

............

✻ I take recreational drugs very occasionally or not at all

............

How many units of alcohol do you drink each week?

............

✻ I drink less than 5 units of alcohol per week

............

Do you sometimes feel you need an alcoholic drink to keep going?

............

✻ I exercise/take part in a sport at least 2 times per week

............

If not, do you feel you would benefit from exercise?

............

✻ I take time out to relax/have personal quiet time

............

If not, do you feel you would benefit from relaxation/quiet time?

............

* I drink fewer than 3 cups of tea/coffee/cola each day      ............

* I organise my time effectively      ............

* I have an income adequate to meet my basic expenses      ............

* I am in good health (including eyesight, hearing, teeth)      ............

* I am able to speak openly about my feelings and emotions      ............

* I have regular conversations with people I live with about domestic issues (chores, money, provisions etc.)      ............

* I get strength from my spiritual beliefs      ............

*I have one or more friends/relatives on whom I can rely/confide
............

## Evaluation:

**Any** individual answers of 4/5 are potential stressors and you could be vulnerable to stress

If you have two or three answers of 4/5 you are vulnerable to stress

If you have more than three answers of 4/5 you are seriously vulnerable to stress

If your total answers are > 25 you could be vulnerable to stress

If your total answers are > 45 you are vulnerable to stress

If your total answers are > 70 you are seriously vulnerable to stress

Let's look at some of the main issues in this survey:

**Insomnia** is often associated with stress and there are many facets to this condition. Whilst some people can get to sleep easily but wake up during the night with their head buzzing with lots of thoughts and plans others can not get to sleep for

> Restful sleep is health giving and nourishing.

hours as they remember conversations and plan strategies. Awareness of what is right and works for you is the key to a successful sleep pattern. A useful strategy is to keep a pen and paper beside the bed to jot down thoughts which wake you up You will then be able to get back to sleep easily.
Take a few deep breaths…zzzzzz

*Food* is a vital part of life as it provides the source for the energy on which our bodies survive. The human body is self-cleansing, self-maintaining and self-healing. It requires us to supply it with appropriate foods to sustain well-being and balance. In the last 40 years processed food has been produced by manufacturers creating so called convenience foods. These contain additives never used before in traditional cooking. Similarly, food is grown and reared on soils which are very deficient of a variety of minerals due to over production and the use of inorganic fertilisers. Antibiotics, growth hormones and animal detritus are fed to animals, many of which are reared in a highly intensive manner. Genetic modification of staple foods has dramatically increased the speed of natural and artificial change which has been occurring over the last 2,000 years.

Such information is regularly overlooked by many in their search for quick food options and variety. It means that much of the food available looks great but lacks vital vitamins and minerals essential to a healthy body. Even eating a healthy balanced diet which involves appropriate levels of fat, carbohydrate and protein, we may still be missing the vitamin/mineral mix which is so important for the normal functioning of the body.

600,000 years ago Stone Age Man went foraging for food, grown in an earth full of nutrients. We face a similar foraging task today - that of finding nutritious food - but from a depleted earth. This is why there is such an interest in growing 'organic' food, since the earth they are grown in should have all the essential nutrients in their natural state.

If our body is toxic from acidic build up of materials it is unable to eliminate our waste, this acts as an internal pressure (stressor) to our systems.

What we eat affects our well- being and our energy. One of the indicators of a stressed body is lack of energy.

When a vehicle is filled with inappropriate fuel there are excess carbon deposits on the spark plugs, parts of the engine become clogged and it emits foul exhaust fumes. We recognise immediately that it has been fuelled incorrectly. Why then can we not apply this knowledge to our own bodies?

eat food which is fresh and free from additives.

Changes in our diet have undoubtedly been a factor in the development of stress related illness. 21st Century life is hectic and busy. In the workplace many employees skip lunch all together or eat a hurried sandwich from the local shop at their desk. Others nip out for a burger or pizza meal. In many schools, fast food options mirror this trend. The quality of such food is low from the point of view of protein, vitamins and minerals and high in flavourings and preservatives. Not only is food gulped down but often there is no break in activity. Inadequate food, eaten hurriedly is an added stressor to the body.

"**Smoking** is bad for your health." That is the warning on the cigarette packets. Much information has been disseminated – in schools, doctors' surgeries, and hospitals, indicating the danger to health of smoking cigarettes. Most work and public places are now smoke-free. Smoking is a known body stressor ; it releases carbon monoxide into the blood stream, affects the nervous system with nicotine, coats the lungs with tar and creates habits which can be addictive. For many years it was socially acceptable but in the 21st Century it is fast becoming antisocial. Smoking related illness affect people from their 30s onwards and these illnesses can be another stressor in a person's life.

People who choose to smoke know the dangers. It is their choice but the practice does infringe the breathing space of others. This can be a further pressure in the workplace and in personal relationships.

use all drugs sparingly or not at all....... they are toxic to your system and limit your full potential

**Recreational drugs** are widely available. They change body and mind functions and reactions and are illegal; some are addictive - all of which leads to extra pressure on an individual and sometimes their relatives and friends. There is evidence that long term use of such drugs produces stress indicators which is not surprising as they affect the whole energetics of the body, creating imbalance.

**Alcohol** is another recreational drug but it is legal to persons over 18. It anaesthetises the central nervous system and relaxes the muscles. It is removed from the body by the liver and if taken in excess, the liver can become seriously damaged, especially in young people. Prolonged excessive use of alcohol kills. Some people use it as a crutch to help them ignore other stressors in their life. It can become addictive and highly damaging for relationships, family life and well-being.

Our forbears achieved **exercise** through walking or cycling to work and growing their own vegetables. Their employment often involved quite a bit of exercise too. If this amount of activity represents your average day then you probably get enough exercise to keep you body healthy and fit. The increase in fitness gyms around the country would suggest that lots of people feel they need some extra exercise opportunity.
Before embarking on an exercise plan it is advisable to inform your GP. A well planned regime in a gym is certainly adequate

but there are many other routes for those who do not have such a facility near by or for whom the treadmill is tedious. Fast, purposeful walking, swimming, cycling, rowing, gardening (digging and moving heavy things around) are all excellent exercise. There are many videos to choose from for those who prefer to work-out at home.

do exercise you enjoy.

Exercise tones the body and assists processes like digestion, absorption and elimination thus enhancing self-cleansing and self-maintenance. The 'feel good' hormone, serotonin is produced during exercise.

Quality **relaxation and meditation** clears the mind and relaxes the body. It is highly beneficial for busy minds and tired, exhausted bodies. There are many books, tapes, CDs and classes to choose from and it is an optimum way to utilise valuable time.

learn relaxation and meditation. it refreshes, revives and rejuvenates the whole person

**Tea, coffee** and well known **colas** all contain caffeine which is a stimulant. Like any drug, it changes the mind and body and some people can become addicted to it. In moderation it is tolerated in the body but excessive intake can cause extreme behaviour, irritability, and tremors as well as dehydration.

enjoy a coffee, tea or cola but reduce your intake to one or two a day

On the other hand, **water** keeps the body and mind hydrated. Our body is approximately 80% water and requires to be 'topped up' regularly. There are many benefits to the organs, especially the kidneys but it is good to check with your GP before increasing your current intake. Many headaches and irritability are caused by dehydration.

drink 2 litres of unpolluted water every day

**Effective use of time** is a great skill and aids a busy schedule greatly. There are many schemes to encourage people to manage their time more effectively –
☺ knowing your most alert (up) time and doing challenging tasks at this time

⊕ knowing your tired (down) time and doing less demanding or routine tasks

⊕ assessing the importance of the day's tasks and prioritising them

⊕ be realistic about time schedules

⊕ batch similar tasks together – like phone calls or paperwork

⊕ take control of your time wasters – people, e mails, telephone calls etc

⊕ take regular 'brain check' breaks if you do a cerebral job

⊕ take regular stretch breaks

> daydream occasionally when it is safe to do so

Clear communication also helps as does the ability to delegate and prioritise. However a little time to 'stand and stare' is also very valuable.

> know your outgoings and income

**Financial** pressures are great stressors. The first requirement is to meet your basic expenses and this factor can vary greatly from person to person. If finances are tight, it is important to tell the relevant people and make prudent reductions where possible.

> acknowledge your emotions and use them intelligently

**Emotions and feelings** are the food for gremlins (see chapter 1). Emotions power our reactions, which can be indifferent or intense, strong or weak. When extreme reactions are regularly experienced, the chemicals associated with stress increase and symptoms follow. The opportunity to speak openly about your emotions and have them validated is very beneficial.

**Lack of communications** about domestic and other life issues (including sex), is very common and often the root of misunderstanding, resentment and concern. people are juggling work children, travel, money and other commitments many pressures can build up and they keep them to themselves or assume their partner knows what the problems are. Although

72

many partners are sensitive to the needs of their nearest and dearest their way of handling the concern is often different and as yet no one has managed to read another person's mind.

Communicate
Communicate
Communicate

It is essential to tell partners, children, family and colleagues what you need from them and negotiate how your needs can be met. Most effective communications result in some negotiation where hopefully both parties feel satisfied.

**Spiritual beliefs**, of whatever sort, nurture another aspect of human beings – the soul or spirit. If beliefs are clear, an inner peace and calm can be the result along with a clear sense of purpose and destiny. The ability to forgive self and others is extremely powerful and releasing.

Thousands of clients and hundreds of thousands of hours have convinced myself and my colleagues that what we think, what we eat, what we have experienced and what we believe, actively influences how our bodies react to a build up of challenges. Stress reactions are the response of a joined-up body which is trying to cope with many pressures.

# Personality

How do you define yourself?

What do you think you are really like?

## Other people's perceptions

These are very personal questions but many people in your circle of friends and acquaintances will have an opinion on them. It might be useful to ask.

In the inner circle below write in the names of the people who

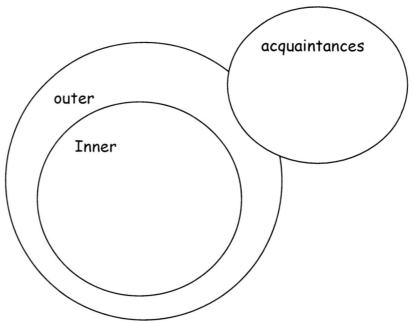

are most important to you. In the outer circle write the names of people who are less important to you and finally add acquaintances to the attached circle.

What would the people in the inner circle say about you? How would they define you?

This could be an opportunity to do some market research on YOU plc.
Getting an opinion and a feel of how you are perceived is all part of your personal awareness. This does not mean to say that you live your life according to how other people see you but it is good to be aware.

What are the qualities about you that most of the above people mention?
People close to you may tell you some of your down sides or home truths which they believe.

Make a list of the words other people use to describe you:

..................................................................................

..................................................................................

..................................................................................

Circle the words you feel comfortable with and discuss the others with a trusted friend or professional to ensure you are approaching this exercise in a positive manner. Remember you are discussing people's perceptions of you and you may choose to accept or reject them.

# 'A' and 'B' categories

It is quite common now to be asked to take part in a personality profile exercise at work, before an interview or as part of a career development programme. Many school children and students are given the opportunity to take part in similar profiles.

This book makes no attempt to offer such a profile which is in the realms of psychologists, but certain personality categories have been broadly identified.

One such grouping is Type A and Type B individuals. Here are some pointers which indicate how these types respond and react:

| "A" | "B" |
| --- | --- |
| feels guilty about relaxing | enjoys lunch or stretch break |
| hostile or aggressive | likes to laugh |
| hurries | takes time |
| focuses on results | focuses on process |
| holds on | lets go |
| attempts many things | paces self |
| reads the headlines | reads the funnies |
| focuses on detail | focuses on the big picture |

We are often a mixture of both types, but much evidence has been presented which indicates that type 'A' predominant people are more likely to be susceptible to heart disease and stress symptoms than type 'B'.

## 'C' Factors

The following four factors are characteristic of people who are less likely to experience stress:

Commitment          Control          Challenge          Clarity

People who are highly **committed** to their activities and view them as important are consistently better able to withstand high levels of pressure than those to whom work is just a task to be completed.

Those who have a sense of **control** over their lives are better able to withstand high levels of stress and pressure than those who feel they are innocent bystanders and 'can't do anything about it'. This doesn't mean that we must control all of the events affecting us but it does mean that we have control over how we react to these events.

Those who enjoy **challenges** and create good challenges in their activities, are better able to withstand higher levels of pressure than those who never stretch themselves and seek to do the minimum necessary to get by.

**Clarity** is the fourth factor. Those who have a clear sense of direction and purpose, a clear sense of how their responsibilities and their tasks relate to results, and access clear communication, are better able to withstand high levels of stress and pressure than those who live their lives without apparent direction, have ambiguity about their responsibilities and tasks, and have no clear communication.

People who tend to experience stress are often lacking in one or more of the above factors in their lives.

For each of the above factors, there can be more than one way to achieve your desired goal and it is useful to be aware of the variety of **choices**. We always have a choice. Sometimes we may ignore the options – but that in itself is making a choice. People who try to identify all the choices they have and are aware they have made a choice, can cope with pressure more effectively.

Now decide which 'A' or 'B' category you are most like and think very carefully if you have all the four 'C' factors in your life currently.

# Character

Here is another way of measuring your personality and style:

On the lines below mark with a cross the position you feel is appropriate

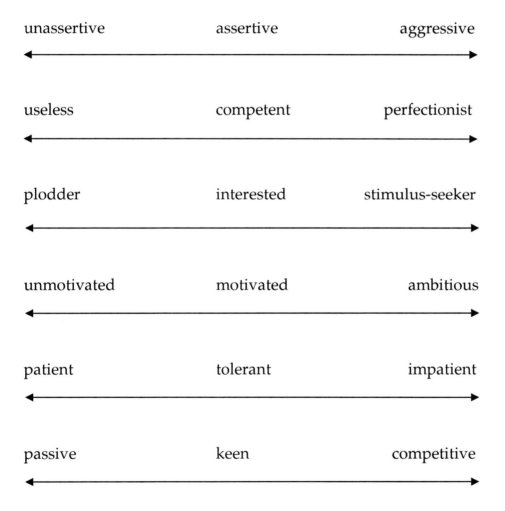

| unassertive | assertive | aggressive |

| useless | competent | perfectionist |

| plodder | interested | stimulus-seeker |

| unmotivated | motivated | ambitious |

| patient | tolerant | impatient |

| passive | keen | competitive |

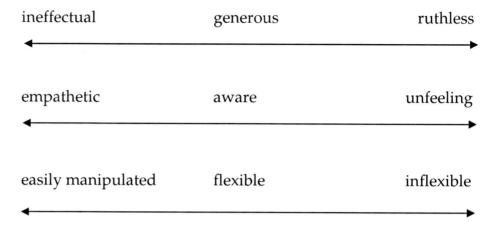

ineffectual   generous   ruthless

empathetic   aware   unfeeling

easily manipulated   flexible   inflexible

The world is made up of very different people – thank goodness! As in the earlier assessment there are no right or wrong answers – only a growing awareness of yourself. If you were comfortable with yourself before reading and doing these exercises then you will still be comfortable. If you were a little unhappy and wanted to understand yourself better you will be developing more self knowledge and awareness.

## Emotional assessment

Emotions are mentioned in most chapters in this book and an assessment has been included in Chapter 7

## Positive or Negative?

Is your cup half empty or half full?
Does it always rain on your day off or does it not matter?
Are you the person who says "I'm not negative, I am just realistic"?

Much has been written about the power of a positive attitude and you can make the choice to be a 'can do' person or a 'what's the point' person.

Some, but not all, positive people have had the advantage of parental encouragement and self belief throughout their formative early years. However all of them have learned to surmount obstacles with ingenuity and determination. They learn from mistakes and have a brighter approach to life than their negative counterparts. Ill health and stress is more associated with negative people and this is supported by the work of scientists like Candace Pert[1] and Mark Seem who have identified the brain chemicals produced in both positive and negative states.

You can practise a positive outlook by re-stating negative comments in their positive equivalent.

For example:
'I never win anything in a lucky draw' could change to:
'I am sure I will win something in a lucky draw soon'
Or
'The traffic lights always go to red as I approach' could change to:
'The traffic lights sometimes go to green as I approach'

The difference is quite subtle as negative statements are often made with total negative certainty and positive statements can enclose more options. By focusing on the positive aspect but with less certainty there seems to be less chance of failure. Negative believers seldom notice when things go well they just focus on the times when their prediction is fulfilled. Although they sometimes show satisfaction when proved right there is little joy in their heart. Positive believers are seldom disappointed as there is room for failure in their prediction.

Try listening to your negative statements and practise changing them into positive ones and see if it makes a difference!

We started this chapter with questions about your lifestyle and then went on to help you define your personality. What have you learned about your self?

Many people are hesitant about self awareness. Sometimes they say, "I don't want to open that can of worms" or "once everyone is told about stress, they'll all have it!"

The above concerns are understandable and can be eliminated by taking a positive approach and encouraging each individual to take responsibility for their own outlook and attitude. Awareness of our own issues, health and well-being is a very personal thing. People who are labelled hypochondriacs are obsessed with their ill health. People who are fitness and food fanatics are obsessed with their good health. The key to these excesses is the word obsessed. This is a disproportionate state and unhealthy in itself. Part of their awareness could be to identify such obsessive behaviour and begin to modify it.

To keep the body and mind fit and healthy we are planning to achieve a balanced state of well-being.

# Chapter
# 4

# Managing Emotions

- normal behaviour
- the concept of distress
- grief
- sadness
- worry
- irritability
- anger
- rage
- anxiety
- depression
- feelings of suicide
- excitement
- love
- happiness
- balanced emotions

===

Debbie went back to working in the Post Office the day after her 'turn'. A few people commented that she looked very pale and she had to admit she found it difficult to concentrate on the complexities of the various customer needs. She found herself trying to remember if she had locked the back door of the house or the patio windows. She was aware of a tightness in her chest and tried to relax her muscles as she sat at the counter.

James was getting really irritated by the constant stream of e mails from his manager. Each one had a priority tag on it. "Which one does he want first" James spat, through gritted teeth. "Head office seems to change their minds every 5 minutes" he thought. "It would be good to have a meeting to find out what exactly it is they want and what the overall plan is. We've all had targets, but they don't seem to relate to these demands".

At home in the evening, Debbie listened to James going on again about the pressures at work and some of the things he was asked to do. Eventually he stopped and asked "are you going out to your French class this evening?" ."No," she replied, "I'm too tired".

===============================================

In this Chapter we will examine emotions commonly experienced in life. However much we try, it can be difficult to separate personal and work life when experiencing deep emotions. In the above serial scenario, Debbie is taking her anxieties to work and James is bringing his home. It is helpful for employers and colleagues as well as partners and family, to understand how these emotions can affect people and how we can support each other.

Emotions are an integral part of the human experience. They power our thoughts, reactions, behaviours, attitudes and responses. Emotions are part of the basic human psyche yet their influence is little appreciated or understood. In the workplace and at home we work with emotions both consciously and subconsciously.

At a conscious level, we respect a colleague's mood or try to draw them out if they are withdrawn and quiet,. When a partner is cross or angry, we can try to ignore it, find out the cause or make amends. Subconsciously, we read body language and energy changes, responding automatically.

The limbic system of the mid brain processes emotions. This is the part of the brain that links the mind and body. It is also the area of the human brain that is the oldest in evolutionary terms. Often described as the 'reptilian' brain, similar structures are found in many other animals. This would indicate that emotions were developed before language and cognitive awareness. It may also explain why emotions are often much more powerful than logic.

People who depend predominantly on logic are often described as 'cold' and others who are very emotional are seen as 'soft' and illogical.

What may be acceptable pressure to you can be too much for someone else.

Emotions change the balance in the mind. When you experience a series of pressures you find difficult and which elicit emotion(s), your brain processes your reactions and one result can be physical tension. If the challenge continues and your coping strategies are unsuccessful, the reactions become intense.

Gremlins© feed on your emotions. If the body is in a continual state of 'red alert' your normal emotional reactions are intensified. As your gremlins become more aggressive, your behaviour may change; you may have emotional outbursts or withdraw into your mind becoming quiet and inaccessible.

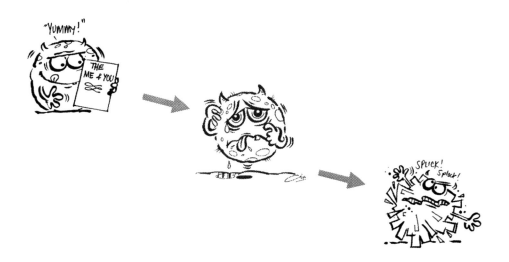

Here are some typical emotional responses to excessive pressure:

| | | |
|---|---|---|
| aggression | frustration | resentment |
| anger | guilt | sadness |
| anxiety | helplessness | sense of failure |
| apathy | irritability | shame |
| boredom/can't be bothered | isolation | unworthiness |
| confusion | low self esteem | negativity |
| crying without apparent reason | moodiness | depression |
| discouragement | paranoia | |

What may be acceptable pressure to you can be too much for someone else. To be aware of changed emotional behaviour you need to know the individual and their usual response. You also need to listen. In our serial scenario, neither Debbie or James are really listening to each other. However if, like Debbie, they have developed a stress related condition and have changed their behaviour, this is a cause for concern. The burglary was one extra pressure on this family that was managing to cope with their current pressures.

In the work place, it can be much more difficult to comment on or judge changed emotional behaviour. It can be inappropriate or intrusive. Changes are often noted in retrospect. Sometimes you do not wish to admit that you are under excessive pressure and will deny you are experiencing tension and pressure.

Partners and colleagues may notice changed behaviour quicker than you do. How often has someone asked "what's the matter?" or said "you are not yourself today" only to get a non committal "I'm fine"?

# Normal Behaviour

Let's take 100 people from the same area and the same age and determine what is their normal behaviour. Some will be friendly and approachable, others will be wary and aggressive; some will be open and naïve whilst others will be street wise and confident. Yet again, others will be combinations of these behaviours. When you broaden this to all ages and areas we have an interesting mix of attitudes and behaviours that are influenced by experiences, outlook, ethnicity and social expectations. What then is 'normal behaviour'?

Anthropologists have indicated that Stone age men and women's social behaviour was affected by their need for food, safety, security and reproduction. These are the basic needs of all animals and we see this reflected in their instinctive and social behaviour.

Since then, over the past 600,000 years humans have developed social behaviours that may have channelled our instinctive emotions. It is unacceptable in many situations today to shout, scream, cry, stamp your feet or just run away. We internalise emotions, showing an outer face of control. For many people this can have the effect of intensifying the emotion, especially if they are the type of person who reruns the dialogue or experience over and over in their head.

In the 21st Century there has been a great upheaval in job security and it could even be the greatest cause of stress today. Expectations have also changed and people are no longer prepared to 'accept their lot'. The ability to change your social status has probably never been greater. All these changes and expectations bring with them pressure and tension as well as satisfaction and self-worth.

> Know what your 'normal' balanced and healthy state feels like

It is the balance of pressures and self-worth that produce a 'stressed' or a 'coping' individual. If you are coping well, you will use strategies which are either instinctive or learned or both and this will enhance your self esteem. These strategies will allow you to resolve problems, in a way that works for you. The result is satisfaction, pleasure and fulfilment. This is defined as a 'normal' state. It feels good and is the state most people are aiming to achieve.

# The Concept of Distress

Human beings and animals gravitate towards pleasure and away from pain. This rules their behaviour. Anything which is not pleasure creates pain in some degree. The degree of pain, in its extreme is distress.

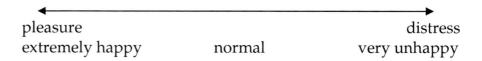

| pleasure | | distress |
|---|---|---|
| extremely happy | normal | very unhappy |

Distress comes in a variety of emotions:

| anxiety | sadness | anger | guilt | grief |
|---|---|---|---|---|
| hate | sorrow | rage | shame | pain |
| disgust | | | | |

Opinions vary as to how many basic emotions there are but the ones which often result in a distressed body may eventually create illness – physically or mentally or both.

Distress of body or mind is a result of too much pressure - often over a period of time. There is a school of thought which believes that every behaviour has a positive outcome. People in distress often ask for help and usually realise that something in their life has to change to recover balance and regain well-being – definitely a positive outcome.

## Case Study

'Charles' was self employed and ran a small office cleaning company. He had quite a few contracts but it was hard when renewals came up as companies did not want to pay cost of living and minimum wage increases. His staff turnover was quite high and many were part time. He worked hard to accommodate their time restrictions and found it difficult to get enough staff during the school holidays. He worked long hours but often felt they were unproductive. He took no exercise and ate lots of take-away meals.

'Charles' was a 'worrier' and had recently been divorced. He had access to his 3 children on alternate week ends and had not yet sorted out a permanent home.

He had smoked for over 25 years and knowing it was toxic for his body, had tried to give up a few times but had been unsuccessful.

One evening 'Charles' felt a pain in his chest, which became very acute and he was diagnosed with a serious heart attack.

After his recovery he improved his diet, eating fresh fruit and vegetables with a little poultry and fish, took up regular walking and stopped smoking. He arranged permanent accommodation and was able to spend more quality time with his family.

why wait for
the heart
attack?
make the
changes
NOW!

Changes of behaviour are often seen in a person like 'Charles' who has had a heart attack - which is a very distressed state. The individual often amends their diet, takes exercise, leaves work at a reasonable time and talks enthusiastically about time with their family. They realise that the business will only flourish if they are healthy and well.

Read through the emotions on page 87 and decide if any are your stressors. You will have an opportunity to consider these again in Chapter 7 when you assess your stress risk.

# Grief

Grief is an emotion which acts as a stressor. When you lose someone that is very dear to you, it sets off a chain of emotions that often surprise the person and those close to them. Whether the death is sudden or expected, there is a sense of finality - an ending of an era, a friendship or a relationship. Some people are embarrassed by their feeling of relief or amazed at the depth of their sense of loss. Many people exist in a dazed state of denial for days/weeks and occasionally months. Other people feel anger as part of their grief process - anger at the person who died, the people involved in the death, themselves for not doing something..............the list is long but the result is usually irrational or abnormal behaviour.

The above is also true if someone is experiencing separation or divorce. The process of grief can be just as real.

For some individuals, grief can be a serious stressor in their life, creating pressure from within as they experience unexpected emotions. For other people, they take the loss in their stride, often supported by their religious/spiritual beliefs or in the knowledge that life takes it's course.

Each individual reacts differently to pressure. Grief may push some further up the stress scale than others. Colleagues and managers in the workplace as well as friends and relatives, can benefit from increased awareness of sensitivity on the part of the bereaved. Time is a great healer and counselling has been found to be very helpful on many occasions. It helps to put thoughts and feelings into perspective as well as validating the emotions and allowing you to realise that such emotions are OK.

> Grief is natural after a bereavement.It follows a pattern and gradually recedes

The death of a pet can be just as distressing as a relative. Our pets are dependant on us and bonds are built up between pet and owner. Many owners find pets are a great stress reliever. Sit for a few minutes and stroke a cat, dog or rabbit or groom a horse and it is amazing how the frazzles of the day disappear. Our pets are often told about our pressures and challenges and sometimes they just seem to know. The energy system of animals is very sensitive to mood and emotions and just being with them can be very beneficial. It is not surprising therefore, that some people feel their death very deeply.

# Sadness

In personal discussions in our consulting rooms, some clients describe a feeling or sense of sadness deep inside. Sometimes they are unable to identify the cause and sometimes they can relate it to a death. Often they will describe a feeling that they have 'missed out' on an experience or opportunity. This can be related to grief over a loved one and a feeling that much was left unsaid or they' wished they had taken opportunities' or wished that 'things had been different'.

One thing is certain – we cannot turn the clock back...or can we? We can certainly reflect back to times when we wished we had said something and instead of just being a bystander, be that person again and say the things we wanted to say. There are many therapists who will work with people to do this safely.

Sadness always seems to be about the past. Once you can accept that it is past, you then have a springboard for the future. Sadness often reveals a learning experience which can be useful for the future.

---

**Case Study**

'Steve' described his feeling of sadness as a regret that he had never had a good relationship with his father during his childhood. His father was undemonstrative, stern and expected great things form his son. He obviously loved Steve and talked about him positively to his friends but there always seemed to be a barrier between them.

When Steve grew up he moved away from home but became aware of his sadness about a relationship which could have been better. As an adult he tried to initiate friendship but his father found it difficult to respond. This resulted in Steve making very sure that his relationship with his own children was very different. He tried to be approachable, friendly, encouraging and had fun.

As his children grew up they were more open and able to share most of their experiences with him but some things are just not for Dads to know

---

# Worry

How many people do you know that could represent their country at the Worry Olympics? Imagine what they would look like…

- furrowed brows
- concerned look
- nervous mannerisms

Think of how they would act…

- constantly talking about the problem
- regularly discussing the problem with others
- seeking opinions
- searching for options
- believing the problem is a reality

And then what happens? Someone moves the goalposts and all the worry has been for nothing. Worry seems to be a rather pointless exercise.

Worry has another effect on the body in that it floods the systems with emotions of self-doubt, anxiety, concern and apprehension. This has the effect of destabilising the normal balance. The whole body works like a seal balancing a ball on it's nose. It moves it's body to accommodate changes in direction of the moving ball. The ball is like our emotions, so the body accommodates them and if they are constantly experienced, the body will remain in the alert state. The result is that the individual who worries a lot is constantly on edge and is more distressed than one who does not. Worriers are often described as 'nervous' people and they expend a lot of energy on things that never happen.

> Be proactive about worry

---

**Dealing with worry**

When you identify a situation/concern which **may** occur, ask yourself the following question:

- what can I do about this **now?**

If the answer is make a phone call, write a letter or something to move the situation forward ..............**DO IT!**

If the answer is nothing................then put the thought aside and focus on something you **can** do which is unrelated to the concern.

Lots of people find the last option difficult and there is an excellent refocusing technique to help at the end of the book or log onto www.strategiesforstress.co.uk

---

# Irritability

This is an behaviour intimately involved with the stress response. It is often an early indication of inadequate coping strategies or defence mechanisms and a body which is out of balance. If you believe that prevention is better than cure then this is the time to ask some questions of yourself. Questions like:

What is irritating me?
Who is getting under my skin?
Am I reacting differently to a known situation?
What has changed recently in my life?
Am I finding this change difficult?

At this point many people make an assessment of their situation and decide on changes which result in more control. This in turn may resolve their issues.

Other people react with thoughts like.........'Get a grip on yourself', 'what's wrong with me?' and 'I need to pull myself together ' but they make no effort to assess the situation. The result is often another emotion .....guilt. They feel guilty that they are unable to cope some of the time and therefore believe they must be inadequate.

Inadequacy is another emotion producing a sense of failure. It is easy to see how the spiral develops as a sense of failure can affect self esteem and this can easily lead to further incidents causing annoyance, irritability, guilt or failure. It is not even necessary to feel these emotions in order...........may people go straight to a sense of failure or inadequacy and the neural cycle is in place. The sub conscious mind accepts this as reality and a behaviour pattern is born.

## Annoyance cycle

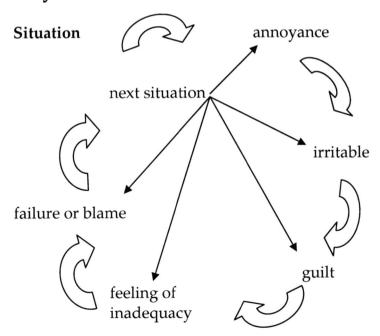

With this behaviour pattern there are no coping strategies - only annoyance and failure or blame. Often such behaviour leads to a victim mentality where the individual recognises the above emotions and begins to feel that "everything always happens to me" and "everyone takes advantage of me". Whether or not this is true, it soon becomes the person's reality and the body is out of balance due to excessive emotions. Regular minor illnesses become the norm due to a weakened immune system or even major or chronic illness may develop.

**Dealing with irritability**

Irritable behaviour is an indicator of too much pressure
- make lists of possible causes
- identify the cause / stressors
- plan changes to improve the situation

If you have no ideas on cause or how to make changes
- have a chat with a trusted friend/ family member or professional to help you expand you options and ideas
- listen and discuss
- make a list of possible options and possible outcomes
- make your decisions on your own, having thought through the consequences

This will help you regain some control over your stressors.

# Anger and Rage

Much has been written on this subject but most agree that anger is one of the main strong emotions. It flares up after regular irritation or annoyance, frustration or resentment and is deemed to be inappropriate in the workplace or social gathering. Like all emotions it has to be expressed somewhere and anger is often vented in the home, usually on all the wrong people. Anger is often fuelled by internal dialogue. You can work yourself up into a lather by reliving an experience or conversation. You often place emphasis on words and phrases which were not in the original conversation and convince yourself of hurt and innuendo.

## Dealing with the public

Jobs which involve meeting and dealing with the general public sometimes result in face to face or telephone anger situations. This can have the effect of catapulting the body into a state of red alert creating tense muscles, increased heat beat and breathing rate and heightened alertness at the visible level. If this is repeated regularly over a period of hours it has an effect on the body of feeling exhausted.

How can answering a telephone or speaking to people be exhausting? It's not the speaking that is the problem but the emotions that are produced from the words, tone and behaviours the telephonist encounters. Confronted by an angry customer or client, some employees have reported feeling in fear of their lives. Customer relations etiquette requires employees to be polite, helpful and courteous but some customers have no such limitations. They are often even more wound up by politeness and correctness if they are unable to get what they want.

Anger is a strong emotion but it has also been described as an honest emotion. This suggests it is a gut reaction to a sense that we have been treated badly. Often this has more to do with our own self worth than bad treatment. A person who thinks no one cares about their efforts or feelings, believes they are not appreciated and this lowers their self worth. It is a very useful signal and one not to be ignored.

---

**Stress Strategy Activity**

People often get angry about the same things repeatedly. This suggests there may be a core value which is being challenged.

If this is a pattern you recognise ask yourself:

What is it that is **really** upsetting me?

Move beyond the obvious cause and attempt to identify the part of you that is really hurting and the value which is challenged.

You may be able to identify a part of the body where this hurt resides and by focusing on the area it will be easier to find the answer to the above question.

---

The foundation of our basic needs and wants is found in the areas of safety, security, love, respect, familiarity and acceptance. If these needs have been infringed deeply and/or regularly, self worth is compromised and anger is often the result

Some people feel inhibited to express their anger and instead of expressing it outwardly it is internalised and held on to. This is the food for gremlins.

It can cause resentment, bitterness and depression. These feelings and states do not feel good and seriously inhibit personal and work relationships.

Physical aggression is a natural response but is seldom appropriate when aimed at an individual or at the property of an individual. This can result in infringement of the Law and all that that can entail.

It is surprising how often the person who caused the anger has little idea that whatever they have done/said/created has affected you and are often prepared to negotiate. Telling them has the effect of clearing the air and providing an intelligent opportunity to move the situation forward to a place where both parties are comfortable.

> A good way to manage anger is to:
>
> communicate verbally with as much control as possible.

If the cause of the anger is a situation it is more difficult to face it head on but telling someone who is involved in the situation is a start.

Writing letters to people who have upset you can be very therapeutic as seeing your anger on paper is often enough to take it off the boil and put it into perspective. Usually the best thing to do with such a letter is burn it! In fact it is definitely the best thing to do, as the process of writing is enough to diffuse the intense feelings and allow you to deal with the issue much more rationally.

If an official letter is required, it is better writing it after your first letter has been disposed of, as the resultant letter is usually much more relevant. This is a more intelligent way to handle anger and has the effect of producing a measured response which is more likely to get a considered positive reaction.

Another approach to anger is giving yourself an opportunity to vent your feelings on a punch bag, pillow, squash or tennis ball. These unoffending recipients of your feelings are designed to be punched and hit, harbour no grudges and do not issue legal proceedings.

A good shout, scream or cry can also be helpful to reduce the level of anger but it is necessary to do an environmental check to ensure no one suffers, feels intimidated or threatened. A place where you are entirely on your own and where no one will interrupt you, is best.

It is sometimes hard to think straight when you are angry and the easiest way to regain control is by shutting down the 'fight or flight' system and controlling the rate of your breathing. Deep abdominal breathing is simple and yet very powerful when done correctly and it is described at the end of the book or log on to www.stress-watching.co.uk. Deep breathing has the effect of slowing the breathing and then the heart rate and this will reduce the production of adrenaline and other relevant neurotransmitters. It then becomes easier to think and behave more rationally.

| help reduce the immediate effects of anger by using deep breathing techniques |

This simple technique has been found to be extremely effective for road rage, office rage, computer rage and all such types of rage we read about in the newspapers. There have been TV programmes on people who drive fast and aggressively and once they have recognised the danger they put themselves and other people in, they can use deep breathing effectively to create a state of calm. They can also use it during driving to keep them unruffled and in control. If they want to get a thrill and an adrenaline rush it is much safer to take some time off to visit one of the many excellent theme parks and go on the scariest rides.

Anger is often the result of a sense of injustice. People have differing opinions about what is just or unjust and this leads to varying degrees of tolerance. In the workplace individuals can perceive they are doing more work than others for the same pay, or feel they are being missed out in the communication system or have been misled. Anger can be useful in fuelling someone to act. They may begin to right a wrong but it may also reduce their ability to view the situation from all angles.

**Coping strategies for anger**

Whether it is anger at yourself or other people the first step is to *recognise* the emotion.
- what does anger feel like for you?
- make a list of the things you say when you are angry
- where in your body do you feel anger?
- does it move around your body with different causes of anger
- what situations make you angry?
- which people make you angry?
- when do you get angry?

Once you are clear about your anger, it's causes and your reactions, it is much easier to recognise the early signs.

Having recognised your anger and it's cause, the next question is: What do I have to change to make me feel better?

You will notice that YOU are the person who needs to change. It is not possible to change anyone else but it is certainly possible to change *your* thoughts and hence your feelings and emotions. By managing your emotions you are putting yourself in control.

# Anxiety

In 2002 The Royal College of Psychiatrists indicated that 5% of the population were affected by anxiety at any one time, but many people do not seek help and this figure could be much higher.

Many clients presenting at our clinics describe one of their symptoms as anxiety. This is a broad generic term for feelings of fear, uncertainty, insecurity, lack of love or lack of self-confidence. These are the very basic needs of human beings and therefore anxiety strikes at the base layer of human functioning. It feels as if the safety net beneath you has been taken away. Many emotions can be experienced but the most consistent one is fear. Thus anxiety is more of a condition than an emotion.

## Anxiety has a purpose

It makes us more alert, more aware and more ready for action but sometimes the original reasons become detached from the response, resulting in a feeling of fear for no reason. Such conditions are effectively treated using regressive techniques with a hypnotherapist or NLP practitioner.

It can be due to a gradual build up of pressure making individuals feel vulnerable or can be triggered by a major event or experience. It is not only recent events which contribute to anxiety but also things which happened in the past and even things we do not actively remember but are stored in our sub-conscious mind.

## Post Traumatic Stress

An experience which was traumatic, can cause nightmares, flashbacks and unease, even if we have tried to bury it. The condition experienced by many soldiers in the past was known as shell shock and is now called Post Traumatic Stress Disorder (PTSD). In the past few years, there has been a better understanding of the psychological condition and this has explained some of the soldiers' anxiety behaviours and symptoms.

Experiences like rape, mugging or other personally directed violence occasionally result in anxiety symptoms or in the person going to great lengths to avoid a similar situation occurring. Such phobic behaviour is the result of fear either real or imagined.

PTSD is still controversial, with some people denying its existence. Such denial is very distressing for the people who experience it. It adds to their anxiety and denies their reality. It is amazing how we accept some new concepts like microwave activity or the theory of relativity without really understanding them yet consistently deny observed behaviours. Such conditions have always been in our society but our understanding of them has changed. By understanding more and condemning less we can start to enhance the life of those who find themselves experiencing this condition.

# Depression

This word causes much confusion as it is often used to describe a person's mood such as 'feeling miserable, 'low' or 'unhappy'. However doctors make a diagnosis of depression after assessing
* the severity of the low mood

- the length of time the patient has been feeling like this
- other associated symptoms

The emotions associated with this condition are feelings of worthlessness, apathy, emptiness and general negativity.

The causes of depression are still unclear but some are listed:
- genetic influences
- early life experiences may make some people vulnerable
- life experiences affect some people in this way
- childbirth (post natal depression).
- some physical illnesses trigger feelings of depression
- some drug treatments and recreational drugs result in depression

Brain scans have indicated that the fore brain is less active than normal in depressed patients and stress hormones like cortisol are higher than normal. The chemical serotonin which induces a good mood is reduced.

By recognising the symptoms of depression as early as possible, amd working with your GP, you can make positive plans to combat it.
Re-assess your lifestyle and attitude by:
- reducing your pressures if you have too many
- finding something interesting and exciting to do if you are under-stimulated
- eating healthy fresh foods with as few chemicals and additives as possible
- taking more exercise and enjoying simple pleasures
- feeling your energy getting stronger every day
- encouraging your self when you make micro achievements

## Support and encouragement

Awareness of depression and its effects is important both in the workplace and in the home. Support and encouragement can be extremely beneficial to enhance practitioner treatment. Pro-active, forward-looking counselling or therapy has been found to be highly effective. This approach acknowledges the person's feelings and diagnosis of depression, then works with them to focus on exercise and a positive lifestyle. Healthy, nourishing foods and awareness of negative belief patterns further enable them to plan ahead at a pace that suits them.

Once individuals begin the climb upwards on this type of programme they reach their desired state of well being quite quickly and are able to take up where they left off. In the workplace or at home there is no reason why they cannot be as effective as they were before or even improve.

# Suicide and deliberate self harm

This is a subject which is difficult and even incomprehensible to some people.
In the workplace, managers and HR professionals are expected to deal with employees who may be distressed in this manner. They are often poorly equipped in knowledge and options.

There are around 4000 recorded suicides per year in the UK and this may be under-reported by 30 – 50 per cent. It is among the 10 commonest causes of death and the fourth commonest for young adults. Up to 90% of people who commit suicide have a psychiatric illness and 70% have depressive symptoms. The Samaritans will tell you that the suicidal people they talk to are very emotional, distressed and often 'at the end of their tether'. This is the ultimate state of 'can't cope' and rational thoughts and behaviour are limited.

People who are seriously considering suicide often talk about it and this can be the opportunity to give information and reassurance as well as encouragement to step back from the edge and reassess their feelings. When talking to someone who wants to take their own life their conversation is peppered with emotional talk about their feelings and the depth of these feelings. Often the word 'hopelessness' is used indicating their total sense of failure. Looking back to Annoyance Cycle in this chapter you will see that a sense of failure starts the cycle again. As there are no coping strategies in place but there is continual failure it is not surprising that a suicidal stage is reached in some people who feels all the cards are stacked against them.

Each individual has the right to make their own choices, even when it comes to their own life but there are so many consequences to this act. Some people are restricted by their religious beliefs whilst others see suicide as a glorious death as recently witnessed in the Middle East Arab/Israeli conflict.

People who attempt suicide and are unsuccessful usually benefit from unconditional, loving comfort and the best guide is to take the lead from them. Proactive counselling and forward planning, in line with the person's values and beliefs is also often helpful. This has the effect of encouraging them to regain their personal control.

## Self Harm

Deliberate self harm covers a group of people who have failed to complete suicide as well as those whose intention is not to die. Self-mutilation can include cutting, resulting in deep, dangerous wounds as well as superficial cuts. Most people who perform these acts have experienced serious life events as listed in Chapter 1. The behaviour is often unplanned following a crisis in their life and is often describe as a 'cry for help'. This is a very dramatic stress symptom and may be due to psychiatric illness. Self harm is a subject which is seldom discussed in the workplace or at home and like all the above conditions benefits from open discussion and acceptance that it has happened.

It may be helpful to discuss with a professional what the individual feels and thinks and working with these emotions, regression has been found to be very effective in releasing these feelings and thoughts. Most people operating in this field also find that loving support and encouragement to deal with their key issues helps people overcome what appear to be insurmountable challenges.

One medical treatment has been agreed, holistic therapies like aromatherapy, shiatsu, reflexology and acupuncture can be very beneficial to nurture the whole body and mind back to balanced well-being.

# Excitement

Imagine you have just been offered the job of your dreams...........How would you feel? There would probably be some apprehension – the 'can I do it' thought – and this would be quickly replaced by a great rush of excitement.

Clear you mind and think back to the last time you felt excitement:

What were you doing?

Who was with you?

How were you dressed?

Were you smiling/laughing?

What did it feel like?

What did it sound like?

What taste did you have in your mouth?

Now that you remember that state you can probably feel some of the adrenalin coursing around your body. You can feel your heart beating faster and your breathing rate increase. A thrilling sense floods through your body which may be tingling

………………………………………..

You have just put yourself into a very positive state by thinking intensely about excitement. Most people usually find this stimulating, pleasurable, warm and buzzy. How would you describe it?

For me excitement can be described as:


………………………………………………………………………

In this state people often feel strong, powerful and empowered.

Sales, advertising and PR teams often experience surges of excitement and work extremely well under these conditions. Flair and creativity abound but it is good to tempered this with reality – it is a tricky balance. Too much excitement creates pressure and too little induces despondency. Nobody said this was easy! Managing stress is about getting the balance right – the balance of emotions.

If you have a task to do which requires you to be strong and positive

- think about a time when you had good, positive feelings
- explore it in your mind
- really experience those good feelings again
- now go and do the task.

This style of enhancing your mood is used unashamedly in supermarkets. It is a known fact that when you smell fresh baked bread it enhances your mood and sense of well-being. The hope is that you will then buy more from the wide variety of goods on offer. In the same way if you smell something that reminds you of an exciting experience, your mood is enhanced by reliving the memory.

Regularly touch base with good experiences

# Love

Is it an emotion? Is it a state?

This is a subject which has been written about by many and like stress means different things to different people. It has been said that there are many types of love. As an emotion it can be very demanding and very deeply felt.

A parent feels a different type of love for their child than they do for their partner or their own parent. Experience of different relationships between two adults often results in an awareness of different types of love.

The love experienced by a baby both in the womb and for some years after it is born has been shown to be vital to its stability and its sense of security. Insecurity in a child's early life creates premature anxiety which can lead to behaviour issues as the child grows up.

> Give unconditional love regularly

Unconditional love is the most difficult to give and the most beneficial to receive. To know that someone's love is unconditional means that you can tell them of your failures and mistakes as well as your joys and successes and the outcome to both will still be a steadfast love. You don't have to be good to be loved. You can be not good and still be loved. This can be very motivating for some people while others feel they will let that person down if they fail.

When you feel love for a person you can sense it in your body and feel it in your heart. It is a powerful emotion and often drives out reason for a time. We have all met someone in love with a definite blind spot! A person in love can climb mountains (not necessarily literally) and certainly thrives on the feelings of happiness and joy. This is an excellent positive state.

In the workplace 'in love' can result in enthusiasm and motivation as a great sense of well being pervades the individual. Sometimes however, it has the opposite effect with the individual displaying signs of dreaminess and inaction. It is therefore a state which impinges on social and workplace behaviour and may require awareness and managing.

> Open yourself to receive unconditional love

When a relationship dies and love is lost many people show all the signs of bereavement and grief which can be a serious cause of acute or chronic stress. Gremlins thrive on these deep and intense emotions and stress related illness can result. No matter how hard people try they are often unable to hide such emotions. Discussion with a friend or professional can help to put the situation into perspective.

# Happiness

This is a state or condition which is often spoken about as an attainment goal but is usually difficult to define. What does happiness mean for you?............
A bar of chocolate?
A peaceful child?
A new man or woman in your life?
Lots of money?
Time to read a good book?

The list is endless and most of these desires and states can change very quickly

Happiness is probably experienced in our bodies as a very positive state. It may be fleeting or prolonged but it is undoubtedly nourishing and helps to rebalance the effect of the negative states we also experience. It is an antidote to stress.

# Balanced emotions

Our body is in constant flux. It is reacting and responding, adapting and learning. Depending on your outlook this could be exciting or scary!

A balanced mind and body is healthy, vibrant, content and grounded. Its gremlins are comfortable and relaxed. It is like a boat gently but steadily moving through calm waters with the occasional wave or two to navigate. This does not mean it is dull or tedious; it is more likely to be serene and joyful, playful and fun.

> Happiness is an antidote to stress

When you are emotionally balanced you are an efficient, effective employee, manager, director or chairman. When you are emotionally balanced you are coping well with life's challenges and stress is not an issue. This is why we need to take the fact of stress in the workplace seriously, as inefficiency at any level of a company or organisation is at least unproductive.

People whose emotions are balanced can be buzzy and enthusiastic as well as thoughtful and calm. This means that they are able to express their emotions comfortably, not outrageously. They do not suppress emotions for a long time but express their feelings, opening them up for discussion and negotiation. Emotionally balanced discussion brings the opportunity to resolve issues.

# Chapter 5

# Communication with others
# (no person is an island)

- recognising other people's feelings

- empathy

- communication

- time planning

- support systems

- maintaining control

==

"Mum seems really funny these days" Debbie and James's son Jonathan said to his father when they were sitting down after their evening meal and Debbie had gone upstairs. "She doesn't seem to want to go out and she had another of these turns again today. "What!" James replied in surprise, "you mean like that panic attack?" Yes, I think so. Do you think she is OK? "I don't know, but she should go to the doctor. Thanks Jon, I'll have a word with her later" said James. They both settled down to watch the football.

Upstairs, Debbie was busy with some chores and couldn't help thinking back to the panic attack she had had today. It had seemed to come out of the blue when she was on her way home from work. She had arranged to pick Jonathan up after the school football practice, and as she was waiting for him to appear she had another breathless turn and felt awful. When he arrived she was breathing with great difficulty and felt even worse that he was witnessing her. He was really great as he helped her to take control of her breathing and spoke soothingly to her, taking her mind away from her discomfort. Gradually she regained control of her breathing and managed to pull herself together to drive home. Jonathan told her how he had seen someone at school have a panic attack and suggested she get it checked out with the GP.

Later that evening James and Debbie chatted about her health and she agreed to make an appointment at the clinic. "We both seem to be cracking up" she said. "In the last few weeks we've both been under a lot of pressure". "Well" said James, "I am very busy at work and it is difficult to know what they want. If I worked all the hours in the day, it still wouldn't be enough to finish everything they want. I'm just very, very tired".

==================================================

Our human experience involves many interactions with other people. It begins at birth and continues until death. We live in a family, which has an extended family, which is within a community, within a country all of which are in touch with various parts of the world.

When you throw a stone in a pond, there is a single circle which extends out creating another circle which creates further circles and so on. This is simple evidence of the continuum effect. It does not just work with stones, we all know how well it works with rumours.

It is seldom appropriate to work entirely on your own. Given the opportunity, we all benefit form some solitude but also from active participation in social interaction.

In the above scenario, Debbie had chosen to keep her concerns to herself but her son and husband care about her and want to make sure she is looked after. Her position within the family is enough to make the first ripple of her ill health impinge on her family, resulting in their concern.

Inter personal relationships are an important part of a successful and effective workforce. Talking with, working with, writing to and managing people is the life blood of an organisation. Throughout this book, one of the recurring themes is that no two people are the same, so it is helpful to raise awareness of the differences between people and how best to manage these.

Lack of recognition of other people's needs is a great stressor in both the workplace and at home. For this reason it is important to value the strengths and be aware of the limitations of individuals.

# Recognising other people's feelings

## Very sensitive people

We all know people who are so sensitive they feel for everyone and everything. They usually have a high worry quotient and show concern for people having a difficult time. Animals in pain, the environment, national tragedies and international disasters are all reasons for them to get upset. These are valuable people in our community as they ensure our local and national awareness of such matters is brought to the forefront. Many thrive on local or national causes and they can feel fulfilled through their commitment. They provide a constructive awareness that encourages discussion and negotiation. Sometimes, however, their heart-felt awareness produces intense personal emotions of guilt, anger, fear and anxiety which are not balanced by other brighter emotions. The result is an imbalanced body which may eventually become chronically imbalanced and stress results.

This is not to say we cannot feel passionate about a cause, it comes back to the need for a balanced life pattern and emotional mental balance which enables us to have a healthy body and mind.

# Case Study

'Jim' was a dedicated county councillor and had been involved in local politics for around 15 years. He sat on various committees and was currently the vice chairman of his local group in a hung council. He was a school governor and ran a regular constituents' surgery. He presented at our clinic with chest pains, panic attacks, irritability and emotional outbursts. This was behaviour which was out of character and some of his colleagues and his family were concerned about his health. His doctor had done tests which were negative.

On listening to his story it became clear that he was a very caring man and regularly became involved in constituents problems. He described one who was having serious debt issues and he accompanied him to court and arranged debt counselling. Another was in need of a ramp at his house but did not fully satisfy all the requirements for total disability. He spoke with such passion and feeling for these people as well as his commitment to his political party. This was a man who felt deeply and when people hurt, so did he. His family was also very important to him and he indicated he felt guilty that he did not spend enough time with them – especially in the evenings when he had to attend many meetings.

In our discussions he came to understand how the many issues he regularly dealt with touched him deeply. We discussed more appropriate ways of responding and methods of distancing himself without losing his need for involvement and desire to make a difference to his constituents' lives. He used the 'boxing' technique at the end of the book very successfully which helped him to work with others without becoming so deeply involved.
And indicated that his heart was functioning fine and that he may be suffering from stress.

# Insensitive people

Not everyone is ultra sensitive. A lack of sensitivity is sometimes described as thoughtlessness or unfeeling. It is frequently associated with low awareness of other people and disinterest. Insensitive individuals are very focused on the task in hand and/or themselves. Other people's problems have little interest for them and they seldom detect an 'atmosphere' created by charged emotions. Insensitive people will deny the effects of stress and soldier on disparaging it as a weakness. They are most likely to be unaffected by emotions and only become aware of a situation when it affects them directly. Sometimes it is difficult for them to react to emotion, resulting in an inability to discuss personal issues which they find embarrassing. Feelings and emotions are often internalised and this results in a build up of tension often released through excessive drinking and/or smoking, use of recreational drugs, intense involvement in work or excessive social activities. Such regular behaviour is debilitating and unbalances the body rhythms resulting in serious stress related conditions like heart disease, stroke and cancer.

# Moderately sensitive people

Between these extremes of over and under sensitive are the vast majority who have a balanced sensitivity. They listen to their friend's problems, offer advice and in turn share their experiences. They will often ask if they are being too sensitive or over reacting and try to balance their response. Concerns are dealt with in a proactive manner by assessing what can be done immediately and doing it. Medium and long term concerns are assessed and plans made or shelved until more relevant information is available. Such strategies result in more control over situations and a sense of calm competence which reduces the effect of stressors to a controllable level.

---

**Awareness of other people**

←————————————————————————→

**Sensitive          balanced          insensitive**

- make a list of the people in your immediate group, including yourself!

- place them and yourself on the above line.

- what does this tell you about your immediate group and your self?

---

# Personal Attitudes

In the past few years, political correctness has made many people aware of language and what it may imply, sometime to the level of absurdity. However, some terms when used by a group of individuals can be deeply offensive, causing distress and animosity. These feelings sometimes result in violence and induce hatred. Profiling of such extreme individuals shows that some of them gain much satisfaction and status from these activities. Writings and documentaries on football hooligans exemplify these observations of extreme beliefs which cause severe community disruption.

These are extreme forms of attitude but many people hold less intense beliefs which can cause offence at a more minor level – perhaps in the pub, around a dinner table or in the workplace. Usually we assess fairly quickly where an individual's boundaries are and polite, aware people would aim not to give offence. However, when you are challenged by a few life events and are well into the stress cycle you are likely to be more sensitive and prone to over reaction. In this state an inappropriate comment about race, sex, sexuality or personality can feel as if you have been stabbed with a very sharp knife. It may come as a great surprise to the speaker that they have caused offence and their reaction is often one of dismissal and disbelief. In most cases peace is made and relationships can return to an amiable level however there are many examples of workplace unrest over such issues.

## Attitude in the workplace

Book yourself on a stress awareness course to enhance your knowledge of stress indicators.

The press regularly report on cases where big 'pay-outs' have been awarded to individuals who have been offended or distressed by inappropriate comments, overtures or stressful situations. Employers may be concerned by the attitude of employees who resort to litigation and sometimes comment has been made on the apparent weakness of the cases brought. When you delve into these cases, there is usually evidence for a build up of pressure on the individual and little evidence of support and understanding on the part of the employer or system. There is also usually evidence of the employee showing many signs of regular inability to cope. The need for stress awareness becomes apparent. It is often other people who notice subtle changes in a colleague or partner's behaviour. When this becomes consistent a quiet word can be helpful but is regularly ignored or the behaviour denied. It would seem that we need educational awareness for everyone of stress indicators.

Many people regularly wail that they are "stressed" when they are trying to indicate that they are very busy, possibly a little disorganised or just having a hectic few hours as deadlines loom and new priorities appear.

What kind of message are we giving ourselves when we regularly say we are stressed? Stress is definitely viewed as not good, so we are giving ourselves negative messages. Negative self talk produces chemicals in our body which feeds our gremlins and the stress cycle is begun. This results in belief of our own negative propaganda.

## Workplace culture

Observation over many years has shown me that people in a group tend to adopt similar behaviours and beliefs. In recent years we have seen staff who are 'stressed' because it is the nature of the job and what it does to them. Their colleagues develop a reluctance to admit they are coping or enjoying the work and a group 'grouse' culture develops. It is not cool to admit you are coping.

| Busy is not necessarily stressed |
| --- |

| If you are busy – enjoy the buzz!!! |
| --- |

In some social groups it is not cool to admit you are not coping. This is often described as a 'macho' culture and not coping is seen as a sign of weakness.

| Stress is not a weakness |
| --- |

Neither of these cultures are healthy. People who feel they can discuss openly, aspects of their life they are not coping with will find solutions and develop strategies which work better for them and the problem has been solved.

## Team Culture and valuing colleagues

There has been much talk in the workplace about 'working as a team' and many jobs indicate this as a requirement in their job applications. But what does it mean?

Probably the most widely discussed and analysed teams are our local and national football teams. They consist of a collection of athletic individuals with superb ability to manipulate a football and develop and enact a strategy involving the specific skills of the players. The team would not be effective if they all had the same skills. It requires various skills – spatial awareness, ball control, heading, goal keeping and strategists to produce a winning formula.

Business teams are no different. They require a variety of skills to complement and challenge each other. As seen in Chapter 3 individual profiling can effectively identify personal strengths and weaknesses and dream teams can be composed. This ideal situation can produce an effective, high flying group who will influence the bottom line of a company. However such groups are made up of human beings and human beings change as pressures develop in their lives. We have all seen a colleague change over a period of months or years as they wrestle with a personal relationship, parental care, or financial problems. This can have the effect of destabilising the team as one valued member becomes less efficient. Usually there is overlap and for a time compensation or adaptation occurs but this has a finite time limit.

The business environment will also change. Mergers, demergers, downsizing and refocusing occurs and the team can loose its edge because the profile is no longer compatible with the needs of the company or the market-place. All too often new teams have to be assembled from those who remain after the changes, without regard to the mix of skills needed. If everyone in the team is a 'doer', good at enacting policy and getting things done, they will eventually come to a halt as planning for the next stage will be neglected. If there is no leader, a team can go round in circles and if there is no visionary, there will be no 'bigger picture' to motivate and encourage the team

On occasions my company has been called in to deal with an apparent 'stress' issue only to find that the root of the problem is based on an ineffective mix of individuals. Sometimes in these circumstances only limited or no change is possible, so we help to develop tolerance and negotiation skills and encourage adaptation to new roles.

# People handle change differently

It takes an enlightened organisation to manage change well. For an organisation to succeed in today's market it needs to adapt to fast moving demands. Many stress issues are caused by organisational changes, that do not take into account the fact that individuals handle change differently. Whatever the reason for change, resistance results in unduly pressurised individuals. Some will cope and devise effective strategies whilst others will struggle. The struggling ones are not weak or inadequate more often they are just insufficiently informed about what is going on and unaware of the 'obvious' benefits that management can see. They are still capable of doing the job that they were employed to do – it's just that the job has changed – the goalposts have been moved - and they do not know what is now required of them.

> **For managers:** build your team to include vision, planning, development, completing and evaluation skills

> **For employees:** know your strengths and limitations and those of your colleagues

Education has gone through major change in the last few years. About 8 years ago Local Management in Schools (LMS) was introduced and some schools were given their own budget. This meant that the school had complete control of how the money was spent – resources, staff and buildings were all under their control. Head teachers all came from the ranks of the teaching profession and very few had management, financial or project management experience. They were suddenly expected to manage million pound budgets after a short course on LMS finance. For some, the pressures were exciting and they revelled in the prospect of a new opportunity. For others the pressures became unbearable and nervous breakdown and serious illness resulted. These were the end products of uncontrolled pressure, resulting in stress.

# Perceptions

Discussions with the police will indicate how several accounts of the same incident will differ. In the same way, 'Jenny' will put a different spin on an experience compared to 'Janice'. 'Jenny' could describe a look as intimidating whereas 'Janice' saw it s playful.

These differences may be due to ingrained belief patterns which colour our outlook on life and set our expectation parameters. If we expect most days to be cloudy that is what we will perceive. If we expect most days to be sunny we will focus on the sunny days.

If you are a very sensitive person, you will notice every nuance and inflection of a conversation and often assume derogatory or unkind comments are directly aimed at you. This can develop into paranoia, when you begin to feel victimised or harassed.

In this state people often mull over words and actions creating their own version of a situation which then becomes their reality. Many families and friends have become estranged over what originally seemed a small issue because no one was prepared to take a wider look and broaden the perspectives. Individuals became entrenched in their version of the situation and repetition both in their head and to other people enhances the emotions and reactions.

# Empathy

Who is the person you can easily talk to?
Who do you turn to when things are not going well?
Who's ear do you bend when you've got a problem?

Whoever it is, they probably have the skill of empathy. This is the ability to put yourself in another person's shoes, recognising their situation. A person with empathy does not need to have experienced the same situation, they just feel and relate to their friend's emotions. They appreciate the other person's perspective. Empathetic people have self-awareness and have honed the ability to recognise their own emotions; this enables them to recognise and read those of other people.

> Always try to view a difficult situation from all sides

Emotions are usually expressed non verbally through voice tone, facial expression, eyes, breathing patterns, body and limb positions etc. These subliminal messages are seen and felt by the empathetic listener allowing them to tune in.

This skill is natural in some people. Through their emotional awareness, they have the ability to notice another person's feelings and not get engulfed. By retaining objectivity they put themselves in the position of being able to suggest options when these become appropriate. Until that time they will be able to support and sustain their friend verbally and non-verbally.

## 'People Watching'

Empathetic responses can be learned but are seldom effective unless said and felt from the heart.

Spend some time just noticing how others are feeling, reacting and responding in a variety of situations.

> ## Try the 'people watching' game.
>
> Sit where it is busy, like a railway station or shopping mall.
>
> Just watch for a time and notice the body language and interactions between people who know each other and those who do not.
>
> Try to imagine what individuals are thinking about and feeling.

If you are reading this and thinking "why would I want to do that?" or "I couldn't be bothered with that" then empathy is not for you. This does not mean you are a hopeless case, it just means that you are not very interested in people.

Practising 'people watching' may help to develop more self awareness and increase your interpersonal skills. It is also a great opportunity to take some 'time out', allowing yourself to watch the world go by.

## Communication

Every time a survey is carried out in an organisation the topic of communication is always high on the lists of concerns. In our every day life communication is essential to get things done and inform others how we plan to proceed.

Communication begins when we are born and around the age of two years speech is developed which enables us to convey more precisely our needs and desires. In some teenagers, particularly boys, there seems to be a loss of verbal communication. Parents often describe this phase as the grunt or uncommunicative period. Fortunately this is a passing phase and speech returns, enhanced by the growing-up experience.

Telling someone how you feel, or how you view a situation can be difficult. This may be rooted in a family experience where there were few opportunities to discuss and 'airing one's views' was not encouraged.

Young people today have been encouraged to offer opinions and seem to be 'listened to' more than any time in the past. Child-centred learning in schools and colleges has supported more young people to speak out confidently and share their thoughts and opinions. It may well be that communication will therefore improve as these people move into the workplace. However they need to have their 'listening button' switched on!

The main concerns about communication that are usually presented are:
- no one is listening
- the place/time is wrong
- the language used is inappropriate
- the method of communication is inadequate
- decisions are imposed and individuals have little or no say

## Levels of listening

What is your level of listening?
Do you say you will listen but your mind is already made up?
This type of closed listening misses opportunities for discussion

of wider aspects and reduces choice. Whilst this may be appropriate sometimes, resulting in repetition of a pattern which has worked in the past, when change is required, it can be difficult to vary your listening style.

> choose an appropriate time to engage in meaningful communication

How often have you tried to initiate a conversation and it has been the wrong time or place? Sometimes we are afraid we will forget the main point and launch into a discussion, only to realise that our listener's attention is somewhere else.

> Get eye contact before introducing your subject.

If you try to communicate verbally with 'John' who is deeply engrossed in the newspaper he may acknowledge your interruption with a grunt or some such recognition or you may get a stronger emotional response like annoyance or anger. The conversation will be very different when he is showing an interest in what you are doing.

## The language barrier

Actual words are a small percentage of our communication system (around 7%). Words and the way they are said, account for approximately 38%. Body language and pheromones (communicating hormones) take up the remaining 55%. It is clear that although words are important, the method of delivery is vital for communication of the meaning.

There is an old saying
*"sticks and stones can break my bones but words can never hurt me"*
*Anon*

In some sense this is true in that we can choose not to let words have any effect. However, most of us probably have an experience we can relate when words changed a relationship or how we felt about someone. It is sometimes the perception of what they meant rather than the words themselves that elicit a response which triggers an emotion and this can be food for our gremlins.

The words and the way we say them can enhance or reduce communication. An attractive regional accent can make you listen or encourage you to chat, whereas a different style of speech could annoy you. Words like 'darlin' and 'love' irritate some people and make others feel comfortable. An awareness and tolerance of such regional and cultural differences reduces unhelpful emotional reactions like annoyance that can be associated language.

> Try to be non judgmental about a person's accent or style of the presentation.

Professional language can act as a barrier between patient and doctor. Long words to describe conditions and illness can be intimidating to people who are not familiar with them. In the same way managers and employees can fail to communicate with each other because terms used are not clear or understood. Use of new 'in phrases', jargon and acronyms can leave an individual confused or feeling inadequate. It is always good to ask if you are not clear about a word, its meaning or its context. Appropriate language, understood by all, enhances interaction greatly, developing good rapport and opening up lines of communication.

## Modern Communication Advances

We are probably experiencing the greatest change in our entire human history with more communication advances every day. In a consumer led society, great emphases is put on new 'opportunities' and new equipment development. Peer group pressure of both young and old is evident any weekend in the stores and supermarkets. Just keeping abreast of new programmes and methods keeps IT trainers in constant demand.

Technology suffers from the same failures as humans : it does not always function efficiently. It can also only respond to the input given so user knowledge and competence can also be an issue. "I can only respond to the information I have been given" is as appropriate for humans as it is for computers.

In the 45+ age range we have witnessed a great effort to learn and develop competence in word processing, formatting, e mails, scanning, texting and all the other developments. Such competences are second nature to younger age groups but we all experience frustration and anger when things go wrong.

# E mail/texting

This form of communication has mushroomed over the last 5 years to a level that can be quite overwhelming. For many, e-mail has opened up opportunities to communicate with colleagues, friends, family and strangers around the world. For someone with a computer and a modem they need no longer be on their own. Many people have taken this opportunity to communicate with strangers and new friendships have developed. Others have revisited old school friends and acquaintances, resulting in reunions and renewed friendships. Some people and companies have used this system very effectively as a marketing tool for their products and many companies now have an e-business department. Intranets within companies can keep information flowing and employees up to date, providing they have enough time to read and digest all the information.

---

**E mail management**

- set up a folder system in your 'inbox' to direct mails to appropriate folders.

- it is easier to find mails related to one topic.

- 'spam' can be directed to one box (or at least some of it)

- prioritise which folder is most important.

---

The biggest challenge with e-mail is the unsolicited material that is circulated and the habit of copying everyone in a group when it is not always necessary. This can result in one person receiving large numbers of mails, many of which are irrelevant. The concern is that important ones can be missed or deleted in error.

Since words are only 7% of our communication, e-mail, which is words only, can be a very limiting way of communicating. Many misunderstandings have occurred through quick e-mail replies that had no inflection or tonal value. When people send e-mails or texts they often use shorthand versions of words and the tone is terse. To combat this 'emoticons' have been devised using a selection of a series of keystrokes to suggest the inflection or emotion related to the words. This is helpful but requires the recipient to be familiar with this procedure.
For example:

| Use emoticons to give your e mail's inflection and emotion |

: - ) smiling ☺      : - ( frowning ☹    >:< angry    :' crying

133

for further information see
www.windweaver.com/emoticon.htm

I recently heard of a client who was sacked by e-mail and
another who was told he was redundant by text. Since these are
life changing events it seems more appropriate to talk to the
person face to face, respecting their status as a human being, not
an automaton.

The following case study is an example of workplace
communication at its worst.

## Case Study

For 10 months there had been signs that all was not well with the company finances. Overseas trips were curtailed and travel was reduced to 'cheap fares', time limits were reduced for work done, often resulting in 'corner-cutting', suppliers refused to send new equipment until outstanding bills were paid, cleaning was minimised, copier paper was rationed, colleagues who left were not replaced, consultant surveys were instituted to survey working practices and there were many imposed changes in company procedure. The company worked in a highly specialised field and some employees managed to find other work. The result was an insecure, uncertain workforce and management. Stress levels were high and illness abounded in those people trying to placate customers and continue developmental work. Senior Management denied any problems and even stated to a full employee meeting that "this Company will NOT fail". No information was shared as to why these changes and reductions were occurring. When the axe finally fell employees were divided into two groups and this was communicated by e-mail. There was no indication what these two groups meant but it seemed that one group would stay to wind the company down and the others would be made redundant. Employees were told to attend meetings at either 12.00 pm or 2.30.pm.

When the 12 o'clock meeting began it became apparent that these people were to be made redundant but when the list of names was read out some people were missing, having been told to go to the later meeting and others were present but should have been at the later meeting. Chaos reigned as every emotion available was expressed by those present. The human toll and the reverberating effects of this debacle are still resonating for some people.

# Time Planning

*"The most valuable commodity in the world is time. Like an arrow from a bow, it never returns."*
*Kim Woo-Choong*

This is a topic that most people know about and choose to ignore what they know. How often have you planned out your day then lost the plan? A great pressure and gremlin feeder for many people is the fact that once the moment has gone it will never return. It is an issue we often work on with our clients, not just maximising time but also prioritising needs in relation to personal values. Planning your time affects not only you but other people. We are unable to isolate ourselves and just do what we want. Many people and situations demand our time and you can choose to be ruled by others or encourage others to work with you. The reality is usually a bit of both.

If you can plan your time in accordance with your personal values, it usually feels better and you get the sense of having some control of your time.

Take a few minutes to focus on what is important to you. We will repeat this exercise in more detail in Chapter 7. It is useful to revisit at intervals, as some of our values can change and develop with the passage of time and circumstances.

*Choose from the following list of values or add your own*:

**Ability** – a belief in your knowledge and capability as well as your limitations ☐

**Integrity** – living within you own set of personal values ☐

**Accountable** – accepting ownership for your actions ☐

**Congruence** – behaving in a way that is in agreement with the way you feel inside ☐

**Honesty** – being open and saying what you know ☐

**Self-awareness** – the development of your interpretation of who you are and how you react ☐

**Commitment** – dedication to fulfil a task or give total agreement to a principle ☐

**Time for self** – nurturing self through good nutrition, exercise, interests, spiritual ☐

**Time for family/friends** – spending quality time with those you love and whom you value ☐

**Good health** – a commitment to staying healthy and well, physically and mentally ☐

**Freedom to choose** – a belief that we all make choices ☐

other............................................................................

...........................................................................

...........................................................................

These values are important when planning the use of your time. It is helpful to relate the use of time to what is important to you as well as what is an immediate priority. This helps you to

> Plan your use of time using a method that works for you

> Be flexible yet focused on your priorities and values and take these into account when planning your time

develop awareness of possible areas of conflict. Awareness of possible conflict, allows you to make a decision and if necessary, inform relevant people of your intentions. This can often save a great amount of time which can be taken up in discussion, argument or disagreement.

Time planning is closely related to communication. Time can be more effectively used when others are aware of your priorities, needs and values. In both our public and private lives there is often the assumption that other people will know what we mean or what our requirements are. As humans have not yet developed the ability to read minds, this is a false assumption. If you have lived or worked with someone for a long time it is possible to guess what their reaction or answer may be, but it is surprising how often we can get it wrong.

There are many books and courses which deal with time management and this is out side the scope of this book but whatever method you choose it helps to be flexible yet focused on your priorities and values.

**Wasting Time**

Time wasting is often caused by lack of commitment and motivation to the task in hand as well as a willingness or need to be friendly, available or accessible. It is helpful to regularly review your apparently unproductive time, as sometimes it has a more long term result. Time wasting often occurs because the task is thought to be too large and you just don't know where to start. One way of dealing with this is to sort the task out into smaller chunks and begin with the first chunk. This gets it started and you can see an interim result which is encouraging.

Networking is sometimes seen as an unnecessary lunch or visit but it has the effect of keeping and developing a business relationship or friendship which may be useful or supportive in the future. Knowing a lot of people, has many benefits both socially and in business. Sometimes they can be stress inducers but just as likely they can alleviate pressure and tension by being able to help or diverting you to someone who can.

Casual chat, either in the office or socially can also be useful. Many people who have moved out of offices and work from home comment on how much they miss the buzz of the office and the casual conversations. Others comment on how much work they can do away from the chatter of the office, especially if it is open-plan. As human beings most of us thrive on human contact but the balance of chat and work can be a delicate one.

## Support Systems

In our daily lives we are often part of a few groups:

- home
- family – nuclear and extended
- political
- sport
- work
- social
- environmental
- spiritual

etc.

> Make the maintenance of support systems a regular priority

Some or all of these groups act as our support system. They may be upholding our personal values and beliefs, allowing us to be channelled and fulfilled or providing outlets for expression and discussion.

> Offer support unconditionally when others need it

Support both given and received is an important part of managing stress. How many times have you talked over a problem and heard the solution as you discussed it with a colleague, partner, friend or family member? This is the basis of counselling, where people tell a professional about their problem and the counsellor asks probing, relevant questions to

> Ask for support when **you** need it.

139

help elicit the facts and the perceptions about the issue. By reflecting back the words of the client, the counsellor can check that they have heard correctly. This gives the client an opportunity to hear what they have just said. Repetition is a very powerful tool because it allows the client to assess what they are saying and hear what it sounds like. Often a client will say, "no, that is not what I meant" and they then realise that what they said and what they meant were not congruent. This enables them to reflect on what they mean and rephrase their statement to create the desired meaning.

On occasions this can be a 'light bulb moment' of awareness, as the client finds the appropriate words to describe what they are meaning or feeling. The effect is that pressure is reduced as they formulate the issue more clearly which can then be tackled and progress made.

In the busy, hectic life of the 21st Century there is much bustle and hurry. In just keeping afloat, it is easy to neglect the support systems which can nurture and heal. People find they have not got time to sing in the choir, have a drink with friends, read a book, go to the gym, and visit parents or aging relatives. We always seem to be busy 'doing' but we would do well to remember that we are human 'beings' not human 'doings'.

In our social circles there are so many activities for children and adults to be involved in. Belonging to some of these groups can be extremely beneficial. Interests and hobbies focus the mind away from the day's activities promoting relaxation and a different stimulus. However, belonging to too many clubs can have the opposite effect. Time can be taken up by the demands of the group(s) and the commitment expected. Surreptitiously the group needs take over and the individual no longer has control. This is often an issue presented by busy and committed young parents. They want to give their children as many opportunities as possible to grow into rounded, experienced young adults and they end up providing a taxi service 5 – 7 nights a week, rushing here and there to get children to classes on time and collected on time. Both children and parents end up exhausted, ill and sometimes resentful. Before this happens it is good to take an objective look at the timetable, the activities and the desired outcomes. When you match this up with the observed results, changes may need to be made.

This is a good time to draw up or review family values and aims and discuss fully with everyone listening openly to all members, remembering that "out of the mouths of babes and sucklings comes forth wisdom". Young, uncluttered minds often offer valuable insights to challenging problems.

# Maintaining Control

### Domination

Most people describe stress as a feeling of having little or no control. When you analyse a person who is showing the signs of stress there are usually one or two areas of their life where they have either lost control or given the control to someone else. In some cases they have given away most of their control.

Since we are looking at interactions within a person's environment in this chapter, it is appropriate to consider how other people can dominate a person or a situation. The result of such domination is often a sense of helplessness, ineffectiveness, reduction in self esteem and worthlessness. This can cause anxiety, lack of confidence and phobias as well as physical illnesses.

Dominant personalities are known to all of us as individuals with the ability to belittle, insult, contradict, and generally bully another individual. They can be a close relative, partner, friend, teacher or colleague. Dominant people influence others from an early age and the experience can extend throughout life. The dominant personality can even extend their power from the grave as their comments and looks are remembered in the subconscious memory unless we actively chooses to release these memories.

The behaviour of a dominant personality is often disguised behind smiles and a soft tone of voice. This makes it all the harder to realise the effect that their insidious comments and negative images have. Children are particularly at the mercy of a dominant personality as they have few rights and grow up with adults whom they initially trust implicitly. All the laws in the world cannot stop the incessant verbal persecution of a child with negative thoughts and images as it grows up and learns to cope with the world. If a parent keeps telling a child they are hopeless at ball games they have no reason to believe otherwise and it becomes a self fulfilling prophesy. There are many variations on this theme of negative imaging and all parents and adults have a great responsibility to guard against it.

A person who is under the influence of a dominant personality is often submissive and unassertive. They have little control over their life and it takes a lot of courage to break free.

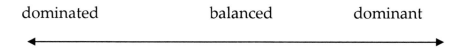

The person who is dominant usually feels empowered by being in complete control. They can sometimes show evidence of aggression with much assertiveness. This type of person will often deny stress symptoms and seem to be stress resistant but the outcome is that they often suffer from high blood pressure and heart conditions.

## Balance

Self assurance tempered with thoughtfulness is the hallmark of a balanced person. They show neither dominant not dominated tendencies; they are confident and comfortable with themselves. How many people do you know with these characteristics? Most people are somewhere to the right or left of the balanced centre in the above line.

Where are you?

It is good to review your position regularly, especially if you are polarised at either end of the above line. If it is upsetting and disturbing, talk it over with a friend, counsellor or other professional to get another view point.

# Chapter 6

# Using knowledge and emotions intelligently

- measuring emotions

- self assessment

- self development

- social skills

- work life balance

===

*When Debbie went to the doctor she was offered a drug to reduce the panic attacks." I don't want to go on drugs for this "she said, I just want to know how it has happened and what I have to do to stop it". She left the doctor non the wiser why she had had the panic attack but he suggested she make an appointment with a new counsellor they had who specialised in stress.*

*"I don't think I'm stressed" she said to James when she returned home that evening.*

*"Stress" he said "I can tell you all about stress. I am under so much pressure at work and I feel permanently tired and I just never seem to catch up. They expect so much from us. I still haven't started the new work they want me to do. I need to go on a course and that is due to start next week – that's stress for you".*

*Debbie felt her problems were very minor compared to James but she really did not feel well. She could not describe exactly how she felt but she was unhappy and she didn't know why. Every time she left the house she felt very uneasy and that seemed to bring on the feelings of panic. She decided to take up the offer of the stress expert and see how it went.*

===================================================

Both Debbie and James are experiencing emotions that are new to them. They feel insecure, anxious and exasperated. If they reflected on their own personal feelings they would realise they are both experiencing a lack of control but for different reasons. Taking a look at what has happened to both of them recently and using this knowledge, would help them to appreciate the emotions surfacing in their respective lives. Stress results from a build up of pressure and both James and Debbie are feeling new pressures – James from his work and Debbie from her reaction to the burglary. James communicates his pressure more clearly than Debbie who may be surprised by how much the burglary has upset her and how little effect it seems to have had on James.

As we have seen in other Chapters, emotions power our reactions and can help or hinder us in achieving our desired goals. Combinations of different emotions can produce new or unexpected feelings and can take us by surprise. Much can be achieved by learning to read our emotions and use our knowledge and experience of life to attain the goals we set ourselves.

**Measuring emotions**

All emotions should be acknowledged. Denial of someone's feelings demeans them, makes them feel in the wrong and causes confusion. Acknowledgement of their emotions, validates their feelings and more rational discussions may ensue.

When dealing with a partner or colleague, you can be proactive and say:

"I can see you are upset, how can we resolve this?"

This type of open question gives the other person an opportunity to 'have their say' and hopefully a meaningful discussion will result. There is then an opportunity for options to be discussed and positive progress to be made.

Another formula to deal with personal emotions is:

- acknowledge the emotion expressed
- allow it to settle or run its course
- assess how you feel when it subsides
- decide how you wish to proceed
- assess the effect of your behaviour on yourself and others

**When emotions are appropriate**

Holding on to emotions which may or may not have been expressed can be damaging to the body systems.
Allowing an emotion to pass either after expressing it or not, is a learning experience but is less likely to damage the body systems.

Early recognition of emotions and proactive management can stop many minor issues from becoming major issues. Such behaviour improves our social skills and as competency develops you will be recognised as a balanced, coping person.

We all react with varying degrees of emotion and soon recognise the level at which we, colleagues, partners and friends function. Knowledge of how your partner reacts emotionally is useful when gauging abreactions (a reaction which is unusual or not expected). Such observations are the basis of stress awareness and a valuable tool in the process of managing stress.

# Emotional Self Assessment (self-knowledge)

An increase or reduction in emotional reactions is one of the indicators of developing stress. The difficulty arises when you attempt to measure or assess emotional reactions.

The outside limits are displayed in the circles :

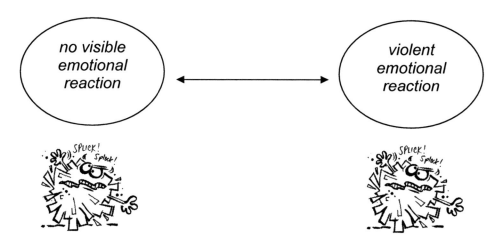

How do you categorise the more subtle changes between no reaction and a violent response?
In many cases it is best done through a reflective process of noticing small changes over a short or longer period of time.

When some people build up too many challenges and pressure in their life they often begin by denying any change in their behaviour. "I'm fine" they snap, "just a bit tired, but what would you expect after a long flight/late train/ hectic day?". By looking at the wider picture of their recent and present life they may notice a pattern of tiredness and exhaustion which is significant. Denial reduces the opportunity for successful preventative measures of stress reduction.

Many people indicate they are stressed when they are really busy. Emotional self-assessment can be useful under these circumstances as they admit that they are enjoying the buzz of being busy and are not actually experiencing signs of stress.

In the workplace an assessment of changed emotional behaviour could be seen as an infringement of a person's rights, if it is not part of a recognised and accepted procedure like risk assessment or annual assessment. Assessment of other people's feelings and well-being requires sensitive handling and is best done through open questions which enable the employee to identify any personal changes they have noticed.

Emotional awareness is still in the realms of development and acceptance. Currently it is best left to the individual to self assess and develop awareness of emotional changes. Empathetic colleagues, partner or friends will often hint or directly comment on changes and that can lead to discussion of appropriate coping strategies.

Self-knowledge allows you to harness the power of your emotions and feelings, empowering you and/or warning you of excesses and negativity.

**Learning to recognise your own emotions**

From the following list circle or write down emotions you are **currently** personally aware of: (be honest, otherwise you are cheating yourself)

| amusement | anger | animosity |
| annoyance | anxiety | bitterness |
| excitement | delight | dejection |

| | | |
|---|---|---|
| despondency | dismay | distress |
| dread | exasperation | fear |
| frustration | gratification | grief |
| gloom | happiness | hurt |
| joy | loneliness | love |
| melancholy | rage | rapture |
| rejection | regret | remorse |
| sadness | satisfaction | smugness |
| terror | tranquillity | unhappiness |
| other | | |

...................................................................................

Once you have mastered the skill of self-assessment, the next stage is to decide how to use your emotions to support you rather than make you ill. There are many tips in Chapter 4 to help you manage a variety of emotions including grief, sadness, anger, anxiety, love and excitement.

You will have another opportunity to self assess your emotions in Chapter 8 as part of your risk assessment for stress.

## Self-development

If friends, colleagues or partners comment on your changed emotional behaviour:

When you have completed the exercise above on emotional self knowledge,
ask yourself "why am I feeling angry/happy/jealous/excited/irritated/.........?

If the result of the emotion is appropriate, channel this into a positive outcome. You could share it with someone, use it to motivate yourself, anchor the great feeling by fixing it in your mind and associating with how positive you feel now.

If the resulting emotion is inappropriate one of the approaches suggested in Chapter 4 and identify which of your basic needs have been compromised.

You may choose to do something or nothing about your emotion but at least you are aware of it. Stress Gremlins thrive on excess emotions and the end result is minor or major illness.

Emotional well-being is all about balance so if you have positive experiences and memories in your brain bank you can remind yourself about these when the results of emotions you are experiencing are not so good.

### Self-belief

We all grow up with a set of beliefs and values which may or may not change as we grow as people. In Chapter 2 there was an opportunity for you to identify what values and principles were important to you (page 46). It may be helpful to note these again below:

Values/beliefs which are important to me are:

.......................................
.......................................

.......................................
.......................................

.......................................
.......................................

When our values and beliefs are compromised we experience a variety of emotions – guilt, anger, sadness, excitement. The manner in which we manage these emotions affects the outcomes, our gremlins and our health.

## Case Study

'Ellie' had a great job in a large PR company and was kept busy working on two main accounts. She organised radio and TV coverage for her clients and met lots of interesting people.

One day, while out shopping during her lunch break, she picked up an expensive scarf that she liked very much and, almost without realising, stuffed it into her handbag. As she walked out of the shop she felt excited and very scared. No one challenged her and she went back to work. A feeling of shame and revulsion rushed through her body as she realised what she had done. Her parents had brought her up with the belief that stealing was wrong, indeed it was very wrong. She tried to put the experience out of her mind but the next time she went into a large department store, although she bought some ear rings, she put another pair in her bag, without paying for them.

'Ellie' could not understand why she was stealing. She had a reasonable salary, a loving family and a good job. If she was honest, her relationship with Simon was less than fulfilling as they seemed to have very different approaches to life, but everything else was fine. She had noticed she was feeling extremely tired and lethargic and colleagues had commented she was not her usually bright, bubbly self. She wondered if she was depressed.

One Thursday she bought a top and put another one in her bag. On leaving the shop, she was stopped by a security guard and asked to open her handbag. The top was found and the shop prosecuted her. She was devastated at the effect her court case had on her family and her relationship. Instead of the exciting, scary emotions she had been experiencing she felt nothing but guilt and shame.

She was encouraged to attend one of our clinics and worked through her experiences, helping her to understand herself better and change the behaviour pattern she had developed.

'Ellie' had compromised her core values relating to stealing, but seemed to be more attracted to the excitement emotions released when she stole goods successfully. Such cases are difficult to understand but 'Ellie's' case was related to balancing the two emotions of excitement and shame, resulting in her tiredness and lethargy.

# Social Skills

Since the Victorian era, the British culture has been slightly nervous about emotional behaviour, Suppression of overt emotions was seen as appropriate both in society and the workplace. This is not totally unreasonable, as people in floods of tears or bursting a blood vessel in anger can create all sorts of chaos. However, when using emotions intelligently we accept both how we feel and how someone else feels. Chapter 5 highlighted the fact that no person is an island and we need and in some cases, have to, work with others. Intelligent use of cognitive thought can harness the power of emotions and feelings that may be experienced when interacting with other people.

### Recognising speech and behavioural patterns

Awareness of different speech patterns helps to create more emotional balance. It enhances communication resulting in improved empathy and appreciation of the other person's viewpoint.

Some people are much better at remembering a face or a place or a route. This suggests that such people are more effective at remembering in a visual context. They store the memory in the subconscious part of their brain in a visual form and the memory is stimulated by visual impact. Such people are more likely to be moved emotionally by visual effects and presentations. They will attach more meaning and sense to seeing or being shown something.

On the other hand, some people have excellent voice recognition abilities. Sounds are what they relate to and it is this medium that can reach out to their soul.

The third sense of touch is often expanded to include the more aesthetic sense of 'feeling', where this means empathising with another person's feelings. Such people are very aware of 'atmosphere' and are usually easy to talk to as they build up rapport effortlessly and naturally.

Most people have all of the above recognition systems but one is usually more dominant than the others. The senses of taste and smell are also part of the recognition system, capable of invoking strong emotions. Think about a smell which reminds you of a great holiday or a special person...mmm...nice. You may be able to experience the smell now, pervading your nostrils. If you smell it in a different context – someone else wearing your partners perfume for instance – it can be very evocative.

People who are visual relate much better to another visually stimulated person. They will gain rapport much quicker as they both use visual words like see, viewpoint, show, illustrate, look after, reflect, illuminate, point out etc., They will empathise more quickly with each other and emotional links can be made. Friendships and business partnerships can result between people who relate well to each other and feel emotionally comfortable.

Auditory people talk about getting an *earful* of *loud* music which they *sounded off* about to the apparently *deaf* people next door. This sentence shows the excessive use of 'sound' words. If it seems OK to you, you are probably predominantly auditory. 'Feeling' people are defined as kinaesthetic. Where a visual person would have a *viewpoint* about an issue, an auditory person would have an opinion and a kinaesthetic would take up a *position*.

> You may not be 'in tune' with some people's speech patterns.

There is much more likelihood of empathy occurring between similar speech types. When you become aware of this concept it becomes possible to communicate more effectively if you can relate appropriate words back in your friend's preferred language. Some people do this naturally and these are intuitive communicators. You know, the sort of person who seems to get on with everyone and really is a nice guy/girl as well!

> Practice using a variety of options which mean the same thing but use the various speech patterns

## Male and female interactions

Male and female relationships are often highly emotionally charged. Sexual chemistry is a natural biological reaction but only part of a relationship.

In their book *Why Men Don't Listen and Women Can't Read Maps*, Barbara & Allan Pease present some cogent reasons based on validated research why men and women communicate in very different ways and exhibit different emotional reactions.

Scientific studies indicate that women have more connections between their left and right brain hemispheres than men. Research has shown that the more connections there are, the more there is fluency of speech and the ability to focus on more than one thing at a time. Yes, that's right, women talk more than men and they also have the ability to do more than one task at a time. This ability to multitask has often been the cause of emotional outbursts from either sex when they fail to understand that both do not have this ability.

---

**Case Study**

'Ian' was irritable and moody at work and becoming unreliable and unproductive. His company encouraged him to contact us to have a stress check. During this assessment it became clear that his work was not an issue for him but he was not coping well at home. He had also given up regular exercise because he felt depressed. He had 4 children between 1 and 4 years and his wife was finding them a handful. He worked shifts and had 2 days off between change-over. In these two days he helped in the home and soon had everything organised and flowing. He described his work pattern in a similar manner. He was very capable of getting tasks done and in discussion it became clear he was very good at multitasking. The issue at home was that he was better than his wife and he was getting annoyed at her inability to cope when he knew he could do it.

Once he understood the reasons for his annoyance and celebrated his multitasking ability he quickly learned to be more understanding and aware of his wife's difficulties and challenges. They both discussed how they were going to cope and harmony was restored (most of the time).

---

This is an unusual case as the multitasking person was a man and they are usually women. It also illustrates how the emotion of irritation becomes enhanced to a level where it affects the whole mind and involves all areas including work, social and home life.

It is not just in multitasking that men and women are different. Their emotional reactions to challenges are also different. Women cry more than men. They use emotional adjectives and talk about how they are feeling. When they do this, they are tapping into the right side of the brain, making emotional connections. At this point they do not necessarily want answers and may have already begun the assessing process and come to a decision. Men on the other hand react to challenges or problems much less emotionally and use effective problem-solving skills, honed since the stone age. This seldom involves much emotion and is powered predominantly by the left side of the brain.

work with emotions rather than denying them

These very different emotional responses create varied reactions in both men and women and it helps, sometimes, if each understands why the other responds in the way they do. How often have you heard a man say "women, I do not understand them!" and the equivalent comment from women?

By appreciating these emotional differences between the sexes we can work with them rather than denying them. The result is enhanced communication and harmony at work, home and socially.

## Work / Life balance

In the 20th and 21st Century changing social, political and consumer principles have changed the workplace and the working hours. Some jobs like mining, agriculture and audio-typists have nearly disappeared to be replaced by call centres, recruitment consultants and computer experts. All work has its advantages and disadvantages – long hours, dirty, sweaty conditions, monotony, light airy offices, opportunities to work outside, stimulating discussion, being part of the development of children and young people. Each person has their own opinion of what makes a good, enjoyable workplace.

Some people are fortunate to work at something they enjoy, whilst others see it as a method of gaining enough money to do what they want to do. Many different emotions are produced and sustained in the workplace.

In her policy document 'The work-life balance....and all that', Ruth Lea of the Institute of Directors refers to research indicating that British workers do not work longer hours than the rest of Europe and is scathing of the diagnosis of 'stress' as a reason for being off work. She cites evidence that the workplace is not an insecure place as there was little difference between 1975 and 1995 in the percentage of people working with the same employer for 10 years or more; according to her statistics, retention rates are high in the UK for short duration workers compared with international standards.

Unfortunately these research statistics are not reflected in conversations with the UK national workforce. This does not mean the statistics are untrue but the perception of the workforce is that they are travelling longer, working later, arriving earlier and the quality of their life is less as they seem to be perpetually running to keep up with expectations and targets set for them.

In reality, companies are in business to make profit and remain globally competitive, creating a thriving and prosperous economy. Organisations are based on a workforce that expects a healthy environment with enough pressure to motivate and achieve both individually and for the company – if both are achieved we have the classic win/win scenario.

Let us look at some basic information. Making the following assumptions about :

Work/travel – 10 hours per day for 230 days a year
Sleep      - 7 hours per night
Week ends - 52 per year
Holidays  - 31 days including Bank Holidays

It appears that:

Work takes up approximately 2,300 hours in the year.
We sleep for approximately 2,555 hours each year.
That leaves 3,444 hours for 'life'

This suggests that work is 26% of our existence, 'life' (including holidays and weekends) is 44% and we sleep for 30% of our time.

Does this reflect your experience?
Do these percentages sound right to you?
Is your work / life balance 1 / 1.7 ? In other words, do you have nearly twice the time for 'life' that you have for work?

Currently the knowledge of these statistics causes emotions of incredulity, resentment and disbelief in some employees and others would agree with them whole heartedly.

The above figures are average working hours and many people today have varied working arrangement options.
There are patterns that focus on:
- how much time an employee works – full-time, part time, job sharing, term-time working and overtime options.
- when employees do their work – flexitime, compressed working hours, annualised working hours, shift work and self-rostering
- where an employee works – employers premises, home
- breaks from work – maternity, paternity, sabbatical
- company benefits like childcare, eldercare, phased or flexible retirement

There are many emotions induced by work / life balance or lack of balance and even some of the above arrangements designed to improve the balance, have been found to be stress inducing.

Find out what your
company is doing
under the
government
initiative for
work/life balance

Guilt and resentment are the most common emotions we encounter in relation to work / life balance. Comments like *"I never saw my children grow up, I was working so hard"* and *"I seem to be constantly juggling children, parents, work and shopping, and getting very little right"* as well as *"I love gardening / golf / swimming, but I never seem to have any time for it"* are often heard in our clinics. Such emotions, if unchecked can flood the body with their associated chemicals causing illness and malaise.

People on high incomes can afford the back up arrangement of housekeeper, nanny and gardener to keep the domestic arrangements running smoothly. Most families cannot afford such help and despite all the labour saving devices in the home, many find the act of balancing work and life quite exhausting. Standards, expectations and house prices have encouraged both partners in a relationship to work to provide the necessary income. The emotions induced from standards we wish to maintain or improve, expectations created by education and media information and the type of home we wish to live in can be a heady mix. Sometimes it can be stimulating, exciting and satisfying and at other times it can be depressing, overloading and disappointing. All of these emotions are what life is made of but if present in excess or for long periods of time they can overload the body systems, resulting in illness.

Assess the
possibilities of
changing your
working pattern to
improve your
work/life balance

Find out what is
available from
www.dti.gsi.gov.uk

Some people regularly react with negative feelings, whilst others have a more even-handed, balanced reaction; yet others, are eternal optimists always seeing the best and positive aspects of any situation. Since emotions power our reactions we can benefit from understanding a little about how different people react and how this affects their response. This will enhance communication at all levels – from the boardroom to the bedroom.

Emotional reactions create the production of chemicals that have a vibrational effect throughout the body and often affect particular organs or systems. This has the effect of causing an imbalance or rebalance depending on the current body state. It follows that emotions are neither positive nor negative - they cause reactions which may be perceived in a variety of ways, some of which may be positive and some may be negative.

## Channelling Emotions

Too many challenges, regularly experienced, create stress. Stress is regularly associated with a build up of emotional reactions. When we learn to recognise our emotions and channel the resulting reactions intelligently, we can begin to resolve many issues before they become too extreme or unmanageable.

## Self worth

Most people like to have good work acknowledged warmly and sincerely. This is an acceptable emotional gift and it is a good experience. Yet when we carry out attitude surveys in organisations, lack of acknowledgement is high on the list statements of concern often causing resentment. Managers are sometimes heard to say "it's their job, why should I congratulate them for doing their job". However going back to our human wants and needs, security, respect and acceptance are met by an encouraging "well done" and self worth is reinforced.

The strongest self worth, however, comes from knowing that you have done a good job. A small personal 'pat on the back' is not out of place. Self encouragement is excellent but needs to be tempered with reality and a check that it is justified. By giving your power to a boss or colleague, you make yourself dependant on their praise to be worthwhile. Acknowledging your success **and** getting an acknowledgement from others, is a double bonus.

What emotional state do you want to achieve regularly?

This is an important question because it infers that you have control over your mental and physical state. This is undoubtedly the case and there is much evidence from people who make themselves walk after a severe accident when the prognosis was extremely poor, to people who have overcome cancer and other serious illnesses. These people have one factor in common – they believe, positively, strongly and deeply, that they can make a change in their state.

People who walk over red hot burning coals and cut glass, put themselves into a highly charged positive mental state before undertaking such activities. For a period of time before the event they focus on positive feelings and engender a belief that they can do it. When this belief is at its peak – they do it!

*(These activities should be done under competent, professional supervision to ensure success).*

People who are in a low or depressed mental state often find it difficult to raise their mood. There are wellness recovery programmes (WRAP) to encourage people to wrestle back control and set their sights higher. Many are achieving their goals.

Other people live in a highly charged emotional state which involves lots of adrenaline and other neurotransmitters. This can be very exciting and often very exhausting. As long as they are aware of their intense emotional state, they can learn to manage it when it gets too much.

All emotions are valid but some are rooted in patterns which do not reflect current life. It is these inappropriate patterns that determine reactions which lead to a build up of too much pressure (stress) and some form of illness results.

---

**Case Study**

'Sarah' had a daughter 'Emma', who was a drug addict. Over a period of years 'Sarah' and her husband tried to support and encourage 'Emma' to kick her habit. At one very low point 'Sarah; saw 'Emma' sitting begging on the street in a doorway and just had to walk away. This image was very painful for her.

After a few years, 'Emma' managed to successfully overcome her addiction and was getting married.

'Sarah' felt she should be absolutely delighted but found she was very sad and the image of 'Emma' in the doorway was haunting her. Every time she looked at 'Emma' she saw the image. 'Sarah' became withdrawn and uncommunicative with regular bouts of cold or 'flu. This affected her work and her employer suggested she visit our clinic.

'Sarah' realised she was fixed into an inappropriate pattern where she saw her daughter as she used to be. She worked on changing the image very successfully and rapidly returned to her happier self.

The wedding was wonderful.

---

Let's ask the question again:

What emotional state do you want to achieve regularly to reduce stress?

Depression     ☐       positivity     ☐

Negativity     ☐       positive peak state     ☐

All are achievable

### Reducing negativity

If emotions awaken negative beliefs in a person these trigger the relevant chemical molecules some of which induce unhealthy cell development (gremlins) and illness results.

Some people insist that by being negative and not expecting anything good, when good happens they are pleasantly surprised. In his book Winnie the Pooh, AA Milne has a donkey character called Eeyore who is the epitomy of negativity. He never expects anything nice to happen and it doesn't. He is a pessimist. We all know people like that and they do have the right to feel negative. However, the molecules associated with such negative thoughts and emotions are also associated with poor healing qualities, and ill health. If people expect to catch a cold they usually do – it becomes a self-fulfilling prophecy. How much better to expect to feel well and get that result.?

# Chapter 7

# Assessing the risk

- knowing your triggers

- recognising emotions

- measuring responsibilities

- identifying demands

- assessing your relationships

- awareness of change

- personal risk assessment

==

"I'm going to be late tonight," James said to Debbie in a hurried phone call. "We had a long conference call today with the parent company in Germany and the outcome is that we have to put some ideas together quickly for a big meeting tomorrow. We've ordered in some pizza, so don't bother about any supper" he added.

"Try not to overdo it" Debbie said, "you've been working late a lot recently or bringing work home and you never seem to get a break"

"It's not just me, everyone's the same" James replied in a disgruntled tone, "see you later love".

========================================

Debbie sat down to do her 'homework' from the stress consultant whom she had visited today and they had had a long initial assessment, discussing all the things that had been happening to her over the last few month. Debbie was beginning to realize that there were quite a few factors in her life that could be 'getting' to her and she had been asked to make a list of what she thought might be her stressors

In this Chapter we are going to review the main factors and stressors that result in stress indicators and ill health. At the end of the Chapter you can complete an Assessment of Risk to help you appreciate where you are on the stress scale. There are no right or wrong answers in the questionnaires or lists. They provide an opportunity to assess where you are at present.

How many stressors can you manage?

This is a very difficult question. First of all you need to know what or who is causing you pressure, measure how strong it is and what effect, if any, it is having on you. The current conditions you are experiencing and your state of physical and mental health will also affect how you react to pressure.

This was the task that the stress manager had set Debbie. As only she could know what was happening in her life.

In this Chapter we will assess where your pressures come from and how they relate to your stress level. The balance of pressures and challenges in your life, determines illness or well-being. Using the gremlin model:

- **balanced** – your gremlins are relaxed and comfortable when your body is balanced and coping with the everyday challenges of life and your cells and systems are functioning effectively.

169

- **unbalanced** – your gremlins are stimulated and active, distressing your body systems and cells resulting in illness of varying degrees.

## Knowing your triggers

Watching and listening to people you often see them react to words and phrases with annoyance. When you ask the reason for this they often find it difficult to explain the basis. Others will tell you about an individual in the past who used these words and they have negative or bad connotations. Some will recount an experience which upset or distressed them.

Some words, phrases, looks or smells immediately induce a sense of joy or well-being and some cause an irritation and a teeth-gritting response. These types of reactions are know as triggers. They initiate a response from the subconscious level of the brain. Part of our developmental conditioning involves life experiences which affect our attitude to all sorts of things as well as reactions learned from parents, family members and other significant adults in our life.

Case Study

'Julia' worked in the home and was the mother of 3 children. When she had a coffee with her friends, she would sometimes hear them use the word 'routine'. She noticed that when she heard this word she clenched her teeth and sometimes shuddered. "I just hate that word" she said, "It makes me think of strictness and inflexible orders and ....... she trailed off with an embarrassed smile and a shrug. She finished the conversation with "it's really silly, isn't it?" This situation certainly was not life threatening or creating any serious symptoms but it indicates how an ordinary word in every day usage can have a very different effect on different people. We did some quick exercises to help 'Julia' change the feel and the sound of the word, making it non threatening and more comfortable

Some words throw people into paroxysms of fear. Just mention 'aeroplane' to someone who has a fear of flying and watch their reaction. They become agitated, begin to sweat and usually tell you how much they hate flying. 'Aeroplane' is a trigger for their fear which is instantly recalled as the mind replays what the fear means to them. This can be a much more serious problem but is just as easily dealt with using appropriate mental exercises.

> **Case Study**
>
> 'Andy' was a financial adviser with a well known company and had recently achieved promotion as a senior manager. The job was great and as part of the training for his new role he went on a 3 day management course. At the end of the course the trainer said "see you all next month in New York". 'Andy' felt panic rising in his chest and he began sweating. He left the course and on his way home his mind was in turmoil. He had never flown since he was a child and was terrified to get on a 'plane. Recently when the family holiday had been in Spain he had driven to Spain while they had travelled by 'plane.
> Suddenly his phobia had become a real problem as he did not want to tell his bosses and colleagues. He came to one of our clinics and using hypnotherapy and NLP he successfully made the journey to America and has flown in aeroplanes comfortably every since.

'Andy' is an excellent example of someone taking proactive steps to deal with an issue which has become a stressor.

It is good to be aware of your trigger words, smells and appearances. These can act as major or minor stressors which all add to our stress scale.

Make a list of your trigger words, smells and situations that induce both negative and positive feelings:

Negative feeling triggers                 Positive feeling triggers

...............................           ...............................
...............................           ...............................
...............................           ...............................
...............................           ...............................

How do these triggers affect your attitude?

Do the positive ones make you feel good, happy, elated producing enjoyable, pleasing emotions?

The negative triggers will reduce your mood, causing irritation and possibly anger and fear. The result is a body state which is more sensitive to infection, damage and mental distress - gremlins at work - stress.

> Try minimising the effect of a trigger with deep diaphragm breathing.

Using a scale of 1 - 5, (where 1 is low and 5 is a high stressor) assess your negative triggers. You can add this to the risk assessment at the end of the chapter.

A trigger can initiate the habit of worrying which has been mentioned in various parts of this book. Worrying is a very effective method of building pressure and concern. It is a totally pointless exercise from the point of view of the end result but it stokes up anxiety and concern which is food for our gremlins.

It is therefore a significant stressor and needs to be included when assessing stress risk.

**What is your worry quotient?**

Assess yourself on the worry scale by marking a cross:

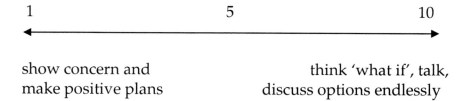

1                                      5                                    10

show concern and                        think 'what if', talk,
make positive plans                  discuss options endlessly

A low worry quotient is between 1 and 4. At this level, the person is aware of a concern and does what they can about it. They then leave it alone until an opportunity presents itself to do something more about the concern. In many cases the problem will have disappeared or changed.

A medium worry quotient is between 5 and 6. At this level the person will worry sometimes and be more proactive at others.

A high worry quotient is between 7 and 10. At this level, the person worries internally in their mind or externally, discussing every angle of a problem that may or may not be clearly identified. Their language is peppered with 'what if'.


# Recognising your emotions

*Man is the only animal that blushes....or needs to.*
*Mark Twain*

Using your emotions intelligently and appropriately is highly effective in reducing stress and has been discussed in Chapter 4. We saw that it is necessary to be aware of the emotion first, in order to channel it in a useful manner. Triggers also induce emotions and you have listed these above to help start the process or recognising how and why you respond as you do.

In the first column In the list below, assess how often you currently experience the emotion.
Rate them as follows:

| | |
|---|---|
| 0 | = no experience |
| 1 | = hardly ever |
| 2 | = very occasionally |
| 3 | = regularly |
| 4 | = very regularly |
| 5 | = every day |

| | | I/A | | | I/A |
|---|---|---|---|---|---|
| amusement | | | anger | | |
| animosity | | | annoyance | | |
| anxiety | | | bitterness | | |
| excitement | | | delight | | |
| dejection | | | despondency | | |
| dismay | | | distress | | |
| dread | | | exasperation | | |
| fear | | | frustration | | |
| gratification | | | grief | | |
| gloom | | | happiness | | |
| hurt | | | joy | | |
| loneliness | | | love | | |
| melancholy | | | rage | | |
| rapture | | | rejection | | |
| regret | | | remorse | | |
| sadness | | | satisfaction | | |
| smugness | | | terror | | |
| tranquillity | | | unhappiness | | |

other

...........................................................................................

In the second column, assess whether the emotion is appropriate (A) or inappropriate (I) as you are experiencing it now or recently.

Some people believe that some emotions like anger are never appropriate and this may be true for them. There is a case for arguing that it depends on your moral values, social awareness, personal situation and environment. In our experience, discussion is better than full blown confrontation, which often results in loss of control. Talking through a reaction is often better than ignoring it.

There are, of course, various levels of communication. Indicating anger is a way of communicating your intense distress. "Better out than in" is an old saying which appears to give us permission to vent our emotion. A decision can be made at this stage as to how appropriate the emotion would be. That assumes that we have control over it. Many of the above emotions are upon us before we know it, stimulating our gremlins into action or relaxing them. Awareness of your emotions, helps to prepare you for what to expect.

Emotions can be partially controlled by deep diaphragm breathing and taking a few deep, controlled breaths into your abdomen can be a great way of reinstating control if you do not wish to release the emotion immediately.

From the above list, write down the 5 most common emotions you are currently experiencing and circle the ones which are unhelpful or inappropriate. These can be added to the risk assessment at the end of the chapter.

Most common emotions currently experienced:

....................................................................

....................................................................

....................................................................

....................................................................

....................................................................

## Measuring Responsibilities

*Responsibility must be shouldered; you cannot carry it under your arm*
*Maurice Silver*

Taking responsibility for your self and your commitments is part of growing up. Responsibilities are often linked to words like burden and onerous, which suggests they are heavy and deadly serious. In some cases this may be the case but they can also be enjoyable, and create freedom.

> **Case study**
>
> 'Dave' was a young graduate who had just completed university. Over the 3 years of study he had learned to stand on his own to feet. He had managed his often meagre finances and developed communication skills in a student house, as well as appreciating the importance of time management to get assignments completed. He was about to join a small group practice as an accountant.
>
> He realise the responsibility of the work and was looking forward to the freedom of having an income, living in a nicer part of town and meeting lots of new people.
>
> 'James' who had also been on the course, saw it as boring, restricting and conforming. He wanted to go abroad as soon as he finished to experience other cultures and work his way around the world.

Dave was ready to take the next step in his development. James was also ready to take his next step - it was just very different to Dave's. Either option is fine, depending on what your map of life is.

Use the following list to initiate some thoughts on your responsibilities and commitments. As well as personal commitments, many people have strong social loyalties that extend from local society to national and international contexts.

### Responsibilities / Commitments

Make a personal list of what you believe are your responsibilities at the moment:

Level of commitment (1 - 5) 1 = low; 5 = high

*Family:*
Partner ...............................................................
Parents ...............................................................
Children ..............................................................
Extended family .....................................................
Other ..................................................................

*Work:*
The job ...............................................................
The company .........................................................
Colleagues ...........................................................
Employees/staff .....................................................
Other ..................................................................

*Self:*
Health .................................................................
(exercise, diet, sleep, appearance etc.) ...................
Leisure ...............................................................
Development .........................................................
Spirituality ..........................................................
Stress reduction ....................................................
Other ..................................................................

*Society:*
Environment .........................................................
Local .................................................................
National ..............................................................
International .........................................................
Other ..................................................................

Circle any which are causing you concern and therefore may become or already are a stressor. These will form part of your assessment at the end of the chapter.

One of the emotions frequently associated with responsibility and commitment is guilt. We do things because we are expected to or because we feel we have to. A sense of social awareness sometimes induces coercive self-talk with words like "I must" … "have to" …or "ought". We saw in Chapter 3 that options can be introduced by changing these words to "could".

Responsibilities and commitments can also be enabling. A regular commitment can stretch your ingenuity to manage and create a feeling of fulfilment and enjoyment.

> Take on responsibilities after serious thought and consideration and focus on a positive outcome

## Identifying demands

In some thesaurus, demands are described as stress. Demands do not have to be stressful but do need to be taken into consideration when assessing the balance of your life. Demands are often related to your responsibilities. If you have committed yourself to join a group which meets once a week and one of the requirements is high attendance, this is a definite demand on your time. Similarly agreeing to visit an elderly relative regularly is a demand on your time and possibly also on your emotions.

> Accept responsibilities you cannot avoid with a positive plan

### Who makes demands on you?

This section is closely related to your responsibilities, as people in your life make demands on you. These can be pleasant or a chore. Your partner's birthday may be an opportunity to take her out for a meal. Her birthday may demand you take some notice but the result could be pleasant for both. Ferrying children to evening activities is a demand created by your wish to give them interesting opportunities. This can be a bit of a chore on a cold winter's evening and do not forget we always have a choice.

> Regularly review your responsibilities

180

There is a long list of people who make demands on us and we will also be included in their list. Parents, family, friends, colleagues, people who empty your bin, drivers on the road, the police .................................................

Make your own list of **people who make demands on you**, with the most demanding at the top:

.....................   .....................   .....................
.....................   .....................   .....................
.....................   .....................   .....................
.....................   .....................   .....................

## Self-demands/needs

As humans we have basic needs: food, shelter, exercise, clothing and money. In the consumer society of the 21st Century our needs encompass technology, designer clothing, insurance, telephones, transport (bicycle, car, motorbike, helicopter or 'plane) and expensive hobbies. We also make demands on ourselves - to be the best, perfect, successful, beautiful/handsome, slim etc.

Make an honest list of your **self-demands/needs**

.....................   .....................   .....................
.....................   .....................   .....................
.....................   .....................   .....................
.....................   .....................   .....................

## Electronic demands

Recent entrants to the demands on our time are the computer and mobile 'phone. Both at home and at work, practices and concepts have changed radically. Communication by e mail has led to the postal service being described as 'snail mail'. The amount of communication by e mail has increased exponentially over the past few years. Surfing the net is a past time and a research tool and chat rooms are another way of 'meeting' people. Mobile telephones are now seen in the hands of 4 year old children upwards and thumbs suffer from repetitive strain due to excessive 'texting'. Huge amounts of time and money are spent on these communication methods as well as playing a wide variety of games.

Evidence is growing that emissions from all the electrical and electronic equipment around us affects our finely tuned personal electrical and electronic body systems and, as usual, some people are more susceptible than others. Unseen but ever present body stressors assail us from all angles. Undoubtedly the body adapts but it can only take so much before one of the organs or systems 'give in'.

### Time demands

Why does everything have to happen NOW? This is one of these generalised perceptions we hear regularly. Many demands have their own pace, but lots of people will try to hurry, cut corners or just be impatient. Time can be a great pressure. Some of us thrive on time pressures, others hate to be hurried, often wanting to produce a perfect or near perfect job. In the case of the brain surgeon this is admiral as anything less could be disastrous. Other people and situations sometimes steal all your time leaving little or nothing for you. If time alone is important, book your self some, even just occasionally.

---

Let your mobile go to answerphone and focus on the person or situation in front of you.

---

Use your mobile to tell people you will be late, early etc

---

Time can be divided into three areas:

**IMMEDIATE**          **SOON**          **IN THE FUTURE**

←———————————————————————————————————→

.................          .................          .................
.................          .................          .................
.................          .................          .................
.................          .................          .................

Identify you present and future demands on the time line. This can be a useful exercise to help plan short, medium and long term goals. It gives you an opportunity to check the reality of achieving your goals against known demands and needs.

**Work**

The average work / life balance today has been calculated in Chapter 7 to be 1 : 1.7. Traditionally, the man worked and his wife and their family spent his money. In some homes this is still the case whilst in others both partners work and the family spend the money. Many people work some distance from their homes and travel times seem to be increasing. The result is that the members of the family who work full time spend many hours away from home. Often there is little time in the evening for the family to interact before sleep, then work starts all over again the next day. In such a scenario the balance is very much skewed towards work. Time for holidays has increased over the past few years and many people have two major breaks each year. This increases the 'life' part of the ratio but means much of it is intensely focused.

Flexible working hours have helped working families to manage their time better and recent legislation on working hours, limiting them to 38 hours per week may also help,

Working Source Regulations (2003). However, many companies ask employees to 'sign away' this right.

An old folk saying is "too much work and no play makes Jack a dull boy"... this is equally true for Jill. We may be present in the workplace for 38 hours but if we bring work home and spend a further 3 or 4 hours on it, 4 times a week it, this is seldom included in the statistics.

Flopped out or sleeping in front of the television does not count as quality 'life'. What do you class as quality 'life'?

How can you include a little piece of quality 'life' into this week?

## Assessing your relationships

We experience relationships at different levels and at varying intensity. The word relationship covers a wide area from the personal and intimate to occasional and distant. Partners, family, colleagues, friends, customers, sales people and employers - we have a different relationship with them all.
By using appropriate language (see Chapter 7) we can improve the standard of communication we have with all these people and this will enhance the quality of the relationship.

### Assertiveness

The level of assertiveness in communication indicates the balance in a relationship.

---

**Case study**

'Jack' was a train driver and enjoyed his work immensely. Every time he mentioned his wife when chatting to his colleagues he would indicate he could never get things right for her and had to discuss everything with her before making a decision. His colleagues gained the impression he was 'under the thumb'.

When Jack was involved in discussions at work, he would defer to the loudest and seldom ventured an opinion. His eye contact was limited and he did everything to avoid confrontation.

---

'Jack' may well have been quite happy with this level of assertiveness and certainly showed no signs of distress. Being dominated by his wife and colleagues seemed to work for him. Lack of assertiveness causes distress when it results in unkindness and a sense of worthlessness.

Where would you place yourself on the assertiveness scale?

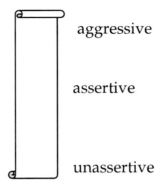

aggressive

assertive

unassertive

Does it change depending who you are with? If so, do a scale for each relationship.

**Other factors**

Professional relationships are governed by standards and ethics. We expect a professional to be detached and have clear boundaries.

Respect for self and other people also plays an important part in successful interactions. This is a contentious issue as respect is no longer given to either age or experience both in the social arena and in the workplace. Respect is no longer a right, it has to be earned and is easily lost.

Personal relationships with a partner are the source of much joy as well as distress. Many couples reaching their golden wedding anniversaries tell us that 'give and take' is the source of their success. They will often tell you that they did not talk much they just got on with it. Today, negotiation and communication of what you really mean and how you really feel is encouraged and sometimes this can be very helpful.

When an employee goes to work, they take their home life with them and when they go home they take their work life with them. We employ whole people not just the bit that does the job. When a personal relationship is not going well, it will interfere with work performance. Similarly, if work is difficult and insecure, the anxiety this creates is not left in the workplace. Both these factors affect relationships - at work and at home.

Some people are happy to be single and may well have chosen this state. The fact that they do not have a long term partner is quite acceptable but it is interesting how many of their friends encourage them to commit to a relationship.

How would you rate your relationships?
On a scale of 1 - 5 (where 1 is poor and 5 is excellent), rate the following:

| Relationship | Score |
| --- | --- |
| Self | ............ |
| Partner/single state | ............ |
| Parents | ............ |
| Child  1 | ............ |
| 2 | ............ |
| 3 | ............ |
| 4 | ............ |
| Other family | ............ |
| Friends | ............ |
| Work | ............ |
| Colleagues | ............ |
| Subordinates | ............ |
| Managers | ............ |

List your 3 lowest relationship scores:

...................................................

....................................................

....................................................

the three lowest scores will be included in the risk assessment at the end of the chapter.

## Awareness of change

*Times change and we change with them*
*Anon*

Sudden change is often viewed with great suspicion. We get comfortable with people and places we know, systems and procedures we have used for a while. However some people would describe that as boring. Familiarity and predictability are not enough. Stimulus seeking people thrive on change and variety. Which one are you?

On the line, mark where you believe you are in relation to change

love changes and
doing something new

like predictability
and familiarity

There is no right answer, just an awareness of how you feel when changes are presented. They can happen with major impact, thrilling stimulus seekers and upsetting people who like predictability. Change can occur in gentle incremental steps which is probably more acceptable for predictable people, but for some it can not happen quickly enough.

# Personal Risk assessment

The following table will help you to assess the risk of stress to you at this point in your life.

The stress risk may change as your stressors change therefore you need to repeat the exercise if there are any significant changes in your life.

The assessment requires time and serious thought. It is personal and aspects will change as your life proceeds.

Fill in the results from each exercise and decide if any are a high (H) medium (M) or low (L) stress risks. If you are uncertain of the relevance, go back to the relevant part of the Chapter and read it again.

Only *you* can decide how challenging some of these stressors are.
You may have others you wish to include and it is important that you do so.

# Personal Assessment of Risk

| stressors | assessment | risk (H, M, L) |
|---|---|---|
| **Triggers**<br>with 4/5 points<br>(page 172) | ................................... | .................. |
|  | ................................... | .................. |
|  | ................................... | .................. |
| **Worry quotient**<br>(page 174)<br>(1 = L 10 = H) | ................................... | .................. |
| **Inappropriate emotions**<br><br>(page 177) | ................................... | .................. |
|  | ................................... | .................. |
|  | ................................... | .................. |
|  | ................................... | .................. |
| **Commitment concerns**<br>(Page 179) | ................................... | .................. |
|  | ................................... | .................. |
|  | ................................... | .................. |
|  | ................................... | .................. |

**3 most demanding
people should be together**

(page 181)

............................................ .....................

............................................ .....................

............................................ .....................

**3 self demands/needs**
which are
difficult to achieve
(page 181)    ...................................... .....................

...................................... .....................

...................................... .....................

**3 lowest relationship
scores**       ...................................... .....................
(page 187)

...................................... .....................

...................................... .....................

**Control of time** (indicate most relevant)

( poor )         ( OK )         ( Very good )

(H)              (M)              (L)

My **diet** is healthy, fresh and free from additives

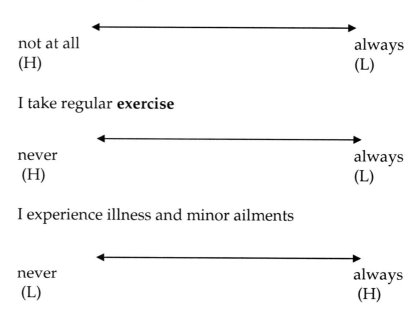

not at all                                           always
(H)                                                   (L)

I take regular **exercise**

never                                                 always
(H)                                                   (L)

I experience illness and minor ailments

never                                                 always
(L)                                                   (H)

You may be able to cope with a number of HIGH risks for a short period of time, but look at ways of reducing the pressure.

After reviewing your results, what is your **overall** assessment of **your** stress risk?

Is it          HIGH          MEDIUM          LOW

If your stress risk is low, excellent - keep working at it.

If your stress risk is medium, check out some of the stressbusting tips and practice them.

If your stress risk is high, take a holistic look at your life (see next chapter) and chose one area to work on. When that has improved start on another one.

# Chapter
# 8

# Life Balance

- appropriate personal strategies

- releasing confidence

- achieving your potential

===

A few weeks later, James had gone down with a very heavy cold, his fourth one this year. He was feeling miserable and thought he was also beginning to develop a chest infection as his breathing was very wheezy.

"When you are exhausted, you always seem to get colds and chest problems" Debbie said sympathetically. "After his exams, Jonathan developed a cold as well. It's just as well that I feel much better than I did a few months ago."

Debbie had not had a panic attack since taking control of her fear of leaving the house unattended. The burglary had touched a basic fear of lack of safety and this seemed to be gnawing at some part of her mind, resulting in panic attacks. She had discussed it all with Les her stress manager and worked very hard at releasing her fear and focusing on the future.

Like many converts, Debbie was keen that James should visit Les but he was doubtful.

"I'm just exhausted by the new changes and everything at work" he croaked.

"Yes, that's true, but perhaps he could work with you to develop some helpful strategies to make work flow better."

"Mmm, maybe ................I'll think about it", he said sceptically.

=============================================

In the hectic life of the 21st Century there are many people telling us to 'take a break', 'slow down', 'relax' or 'chill out'. These are usually people who care about us - mother, father, partner, children or friends. It is seldom your boss, your customers or your suppliers. As a 'human resource' you are employed to perform tasks to a set of standards and achieve goals usually set by other people.

To function effectively a machine requires parts that fit well together, move smoothly and are well lubricated. Humans are not very different in that they need a balanced body and mind. It would be easy if it was just a matter of checking the efficiency and ensuring there was enough oil but the human being is a complex balance of chemistry, biology, physics and life energy. To achieve any level of efficiency we need balance. If we are being told to 'slow down', we must be going to fast. If we are told to 'relax', we must be very tense. The ideal working state is between these limits.

## Appropriate personal strategies

To achieve balance in your life suggests there will be highs and lows. When you sit on a swing you experience little movement. It requires some effort to get it going and then you experience gentle movement. It is the whole experience that is pleasant. Only when the arc becomes more extreme does it become uncomfortable. Now we know that lots of people love fun rides, which incorporate massive swings, but they would probably not wish to spend their life on them. Once in a while is usually enough! Highs and lows are part of life and people develop strategies to manage them, spending the remaining time swinging gently and comfortably.

Reflect on your everyday life. If it was displayed on an emotional graph it could look like this:

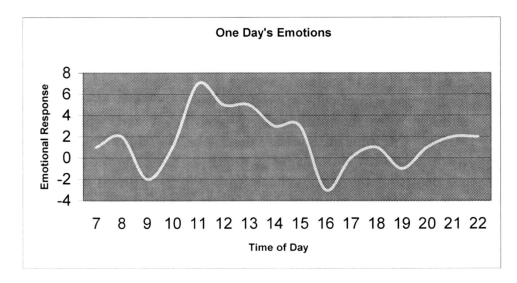

**One Day's Emotions**

On this particular day we have charted, there are more positive responses than negative ones with the morning and early afternoon being spent in a very positive mood. This changes around 4pm with a very negative response, eventually settling over the evening.

When your emotional graph changes and there are lots of highs, or lows, it is good to check what is causing them. The risk assessment in Chapter 8 will help you to identify your stressors and you probably know what is putting you in a good mood. You can then plan appropriate coping strategies **within the context of your whole life**.

There are 8 areas of your life to consider and these are indicated in the circle.

Circle of life

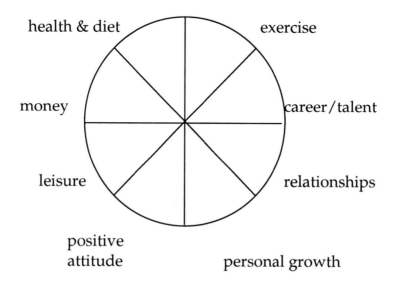

This is a useful exercise used by many coaches and personal development trainers. In the circle, the centre is 0 and the perimeter is 10. For each life sector, rank your level of satisfaction where 0 = low and 10 = high. Draw a curved line across the sector to create your limit.

This exercise was carried out with 'Bill' whose case study follows:

**Case study**

When 'Bill' visited our centre he was exhausted – mentally and physically. He was a senior manager in industry and seemed to be a 'high flier'. He felt unable to cope and was afraid he would lose his job as he was falling behind with targets and general work standard. He had been tipped for a place on the Board and this had led him to show his worth by taking on a large extra project.

He was a strong personality and able to manage his staff well as his communication skills were good. However the project was not going well and he seemed to be unable to pull it back on track and focus on the relevant issues.

After an assessment of his whole life it became obvious he had two other demands on his time and thoughts. His partner had just gone back to work as a teacher 3 years after the birth of their second child and was spending long hours on preparation and marking. She was tired and their relationship seemed distant. The children had settled into their nursery but the youngest had a health problem that required regular hospital attendance. 'Bill' was taking much more responsibility for the child-care arrangements and hospital appointments than before. He was very uncomfortable in hospitals and found these visits very challenging.

'Bill's' circle looked like this:

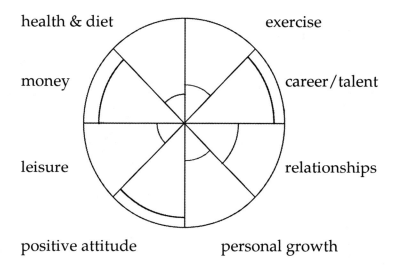

health & diet          exercise

money                  career/talent

leisure                relationships

positive attitude      personal growth

'Bill's' career, money and attitude were healthy and comfortable, but the other areas of his life were low scores. He could see immediately how his personal life was undernourished and unfulfilling resulting in an imbalance with the positive areas of his life.

It is not necessary for all the sectors to be the same but this exercise helps you identify imbalances in your life and you can then choose what, if anything, you wish to change.

What is your circle like?

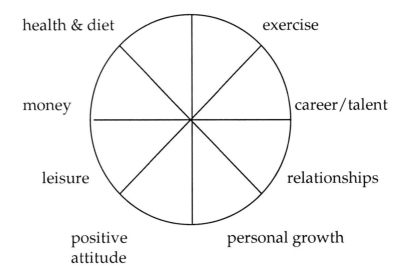

**Support**

Having decided you have a problem or issue to deal with, accepting support is sometimes one of the most difficult things to do. What is the reason for this?

These are just a few of the reasons regularly given for not asking for help:

John believes he is a man and has to be strong; asking for help is weak.

Sasha thinks no one will take her seriously and isn't sure she can talk about it anyway.

Billy doesn't like talking about his health and is afraid it might be embarrassing or serious.

Sam hopes if she just ignores it, her problem will go away.

Geoff says "if they wanted to help me they would have offered already"

Help and support are often available from family, friends and colleagues and some companies offer their employees a 'crisis' help line. There are counsellors, psychotherapists, doctors, complementary therapists, coaches, self help groups, and information centres for financial advice and legal support.

However you have to **want** their help and many people leave it very late before they ask for help. Burn-out, nervous breakdown, inability to cope, heart attack – however you want to describe a serious stress response, often requires medical and psychological intervention as well as a holistic look at the causes. From there a plan, conducive with the client's health, will stimulate and motivate them to make changes and reduce the cause(s) of the stress. A change in attitude can have a significant effect on personal coping strategies.

**Case Study**

The company that 'Bob' worked for was in a very competitive market and he was Director in charge of the Human Resource Department. They had a staff of 1500 and recently had made 450 redundant. This was a traumatic time for 'Bob' and his staff. They were working with our company to manage the redundancies and we noticed that tensions were developing not only within the company but particularly in the HR Department. We suggested some strategies but these were declined with a comment of "we're fine". The crunch came when the Director himself was made redundant and his defences broke under this final excessive pressure.

'Bob's' doctor diagnosed a nervous breakdown and only then was 'Bob' prepared to look honestly at his reactions and attitudes and make an assessment of how to move forwards.

### Reciprocate Support

As well as getting support, it is good to redress the balance by offering support to other people or groups in another part of society. There is an old saying "what goes around, comes around" and another similar sentiment from the Bible 'do unto others as you wish to be done to'.

Many people report humility and increased awareness when they reach out to another being to share their precious time and resources for no apparent gain.

# Releasing confidence

Lack of confidence features on the assessment forms of 75% of the clients who visit our centres. This would indicate that confidence is an issue for many people today.

William Pitt wrote in the 18th Century......

*Confidence is a plant of slow growth in an aged bosom*

-suggesting it is the prerogative of old age.

Observations today in schools, colleges and universities would not bear this out. Many young people exhibit quiet and sometimes noisy confidence in themselves and their abilities. This is encouraged through the many opportunities open to them in school, in the community, with parents and 'gap' year travel.

Many young people learn independence much earlier than in years past and for many, confidence develops from the knowledge of a safe and loving home. For others, confidence comes from a strong belief in themselves and their abilities, however sometimes this is displayed as arrogance.

Confidence is lost when a person no longer believes in himself or herself.

---

**Case Study:**

'Sanjay' did enough at school to get some 'A' levels and went to college to study computing. He discovered he had a great aptitude for the subject and did very well. He got a job in 'the City' (London) with an international bank and was soon earning lots of money and his skills were greatly valued.

He decided to become self employed and took on contracts and special projects. This involved a very different style of work. He was working on his own rather than in a team and often felt isolated even within the IT department. He lacked involvement in the 'big picture' of the projects he was working on and began to doubt himself and his ability. Soon he found he was unable to organise his day and projects were beginning to fall behind expected dates. He described himself as depressed.

---

'Sanjay' had not lost his confidence, he had just misplaced it. Although he told me the above story, he did not realise what had happened to him until he looked at the sequences carefully.

Realisation of the effect of the different style of working, was a great relief. He began to understand what he was missing and what he needed to work effectively. He made changes and his confidence and abilities returned.

The solutions to many of the case studies in this book seem obvious when you read the story, but when you are living it, it is quite a different matter. You are blinkered by detail and it can be hard to get a clear picture. You are bombarded by the noise and haste of everyday living and you feel as if you are on an eternal treadmill

# Achieving your potential

Many people travel through life without realising their full potential. This may or may not affect their confidence. It is certainly the cause of regret for some as they visualise how things could have been if ..............................
But we hold the answers within ourselves and we also have the power to release our potential if we wish.

There was a TV series recently, which offered well known actors and actresses the opportunity to develop a skill they had never entertained. These skills ranged from opera singing to riding in a polo match in front of a real audience. Watching the development of these people was fascinating as they displayed their fears and difficulties as well as their determination to achieve the best they could in the time given with their own resources. The results were superb and a great testimonial to their grit and determination.

There are times in our life, when we have to look beyond our comfort zone, into areas we may have little or no experience. It is surprising how we find abilities and skills we were unaware of.

Our education system is based on logic and linguistics, and puts great store by these abilities but there are many forms of intelligence. In 1993 the theory of multiple intelligences was presented by Professor Howard Gardner,. He suggested that there was more to intelligence than logic and linguistic ability. Gardner presented 7 intelligences or aptitudes which have been developed by many others. In our work we assess 20 aptitudes only 12 of which are assessed in schools. This encourages us to look wider and encourage people to value their vocational skills and personal abilities. The child who 'could do better' often does, using their entrepreneurial skills to set up a successful business.

## Coaching

Self belief and a positive attitude are fundamental to achieving your goals. Belief that you can achieve a goal is powerful and motivating. Often difficult and important decisions have to be made. There are many benefits to discussing these with an informed but dispassionate outsider. Coaching can provide such a person. Your coach can provide support when decisions are being explored and assessed. He/she will ask pointed and relevant questions enabling many options to be discussed and assessed. A clear, future plan is also discussed and the plan can be amended as circumstances require. Sharing thoughts, feelings and emotions with a detached but empathetic professional who wants you to be the best you can be, is very liberating.

Our experience indicates that awareness of all your abilities releases confidence, reduces stress and develops self esteem. Encouragement makes life exciting and fun. You hold the key to your future, use it wisely and listen to your intuition.

| Find out about Coaching to decide if it could be useful. |

# 'Boxing' technique

**Some people have a problem** with an irritating worry, distracting thought or similar difficulty which they are not ready to release. They find they continually think about the person or situation and it seriously interferes with everyday living/working.

**It can be useful** to help them to 'box' this distraction, allowing them to deal with it at a more convenient time. This is used very effectively for athletes as part of their preparation for an event but can also be successful for anyone wishing to set aside a problem and 'give their subconscious brain a rest'.

**There are many variations** but the following visualisation technique works well.
After doing it a few times you can shorten it to suit.

Sit comfortably with legs uncrossed and arms relaxed.

**Take a good deep breath** in through your nose, all the way down to your abdomen and slowly breathe it out through your mouth. Repeat this a few times until you feel your body beginning to relax. Focus on your breathing, feeling the breath moving in and out of your body, sensing the taste in your mouth and hearing the sound of your natural biological rhythms...............
**Imagine** you are entering a room ..........you can feel the carpet beneath your feet and there is a warm comforting smell of lightly polished furniture. There is a window in the room and you move towards it where you see a desk and a chair. You sit down on the chair and make your self comfortable as you look out of the window.....
Notice what season it is, notice the colours of the flowers, shrubs and trees.............the window is slightly open and you can smell the freshness of the day. You can see and hear some birds in a tree calling to one another, trilling their own tune...............You bring your awareness back into the room and notice a piece of white paper and a pen on the desk in front of you.................You pick up the pen and

begin to write down the thought/experience/etc which has been concerning you.

You can feel the pen moving on the paper and the words as they are formed………

When you have finished writing, you fold the paper in half and then in half again…….

You turn around in the chair and notice a large box with a lid. Observe the colour and shape of the box……………..You get up and lift the lid off the box and place the paper in the box and replace the lid……………………..You then take the box and place it on a high shelf or a dark corner of the room and walk back to the chair, sitting down…………………….You look out of the window again and notice any changes which have happened since you looked last…………………………………..

You get up from the chair and walk out of the room taking a nice deep breath and breathing out knowing you have boxed your problem and can take it out when **you** wish………….

# The best technique in the world!

## Is DEEP diaphragmatic BREATHING

How to do it consciously:

- Place your hand on your mid rift, just above your waist.
- Take a nice big deep breath in through your nose and be aware that your hand is being pushed outwards.
- This is often described as' breathing into your stomach or abdomen'.
- Breathe out through your mouth with an audible sound.
- Allow the exhale to continue for as long as possible
- Check that your shoulders are not raised and tense.

**REPEAT** at least 5 times

Check your shoulders are relaxed and the breath is going into the abdominal area.

By focusing on the act of breathing for a short time - feeling the air move in and out, hearing the sound of your exhale and inhale – this allows you to clear your mind and become more perceptive and aware after the exercise.

For more strategies and information about gremlins log on to
www.stress-watching.co.uk
or email
gremlins@stress-watching.co.uk

Printed in the United Kingdom by
Lightning Source UK Ltd., Milton Keynes
137316UK00002B/169/A

9 781845 490201